# MY TWO SOUTHS

BLENDING THE FLAVORS OF INDIA INTO A SOUTHERN KITCHEN

# MY TWO SOUTHS

## BLENDING THE FLAVORS OF INDIA INTO A SOUTHERN KITCHEN

ASHA GOMEZ

*with* MARTHA HALL FOOSE

RUNNING PRESS
PHILADELPHIA · LONDON

Published by Running Press,
An Imprint of Perseus Books, a Division of PBG Publishing, LLC,
A Subsidiary of Hachette Book Group, Inc.

Books published by Running Press are available at special discounts for bulk purchases in the United States by corporations, institutions, and other organizations. For more information, please contact the Special Markets Department at the Perseus Books Group, 2300 Chestnut Street, Suite 200, Philadelphia, PA 19103, or call (800) 810-4145, ext. 5000, or e-mail special.markets@perseusbooks.com.

ISBN 978-0-7624-5783-0
Library of Congress Control Number: 2016941856

E-book ISBN 978-0-7624-5829-5

9  8  7  6  5  4  3  2  1
Digit on the right indicates the number of this printing

Cover and interior design by Susan Van Horn
Edited by Jennifer Kasius
Typography: Brandon, Burford, and Filosofia

Running Press Book Publishers
2300 Chestnut Street
Philadelphia, PA 19103-4371

Visit us on the web!
www.offthemenublog.com

*For my brother Joy Gomez. He has been my champion and defender. His unwavering support has been there whether I was navigating rough seas or riding the crest of a wave. He is equal parts confidant, guide, and mentor.*
*I love you, Joy.*

# contents

# introduction

*I call my style of cuisine "two Souths cooking." Its flavors and dishes are characterized and rooted in my deep affection for the resourcefulness and soulfulness of cooking in both my mother country India, in the far southern state of Kerala, and my chosen home in America's southern, culinary-savvy city of Atlanta, Georgia.*

This collection of recipes brings together the culinary roots of two special places where genuine hospitality and meaning are crucial ingredients. These two Souths are over nine thousand miles apart and would seem to be in separate universes. Surprisingly, I have found their shared aspects—a warm, humid climate, abundant produce varieties, expanses of rice acreage, and busy coastal communities along with a spirit of sharing, a gift for entertaining and storytelling, a talent for creating bounty out of an often modest pantry, and a sincere embrace of simplicity—blend easily in my South by South cuisine. These combined southern cultures, which value gathering family and friends around a festive table, and my abiding appreciation of the expressive capabilities of cherished foods are the touchstones of my cuisine.

My family's homestead was a bustling community of three houses surrounded by banana plants, papaya trees, and coconut palms located steps away from the Arabian Sea. In Kerala it is not uncommon for land to be distributed among siblings, who then build houses in close proximity to one another and enclose them with a common fence. My maternal grandmother's name was Carmel, hence our covey of homes came to be known as Carmel Compound. Brought up among a passel of fourteen children, I was the first girl and, therefore, doted on by a loving assortment of aunts, uncles, cousins, and brothers, all of whom praised me for my polite manners and good grades as well as admonished me for stealing baskets of fruits and hopping fences.

When I wasn't climbing trees to sample their luscious edible treasures, I loved to spend time with my mother and three aunts in a kitchen set apart from the back of the house. Both tradition and innovation reigned in that kitchen. Under the tutelage of these loving women, I absorbed lessons in preparing traditional, coastal Keralan fare. Often charged with preparing the spices needed for a specific dish, I found the daily array of freshly roasted selections mesmerizing. I became fluent in the vocabulary of spices—their names, their flavors, and the feelings they evoked. Just as descriptive words enhance a story, I learned that black pepper, cumin, coriander, fenugreek, turmeric, cinnamon, clove, nutmeg, star anise, and mustard seeds can add expression to a dish and speak the flavors of a particular season of the year.

Spices direct from the market were always ground by hand with either a mortar and pestle or a *batu giling* (a sort of fat rolling pin of undressed granite rolled over a thick, flat granite slab) in Carmel Compound's kitchen. Enticing aromas from pungent seasonings like *kodampuli*, asafoetida, and *cambogia* arose from cast-iron griddles and clay cooking pots, flavoring the air and the conversations of my female relatives, as they navigated me through the intricacies of using seasoning combinations to perfectly enhance a dish. Spices sizzled and simmered over a fire fed with wood and the husks left from grating coconut. My enthusiasm and confidence grew as I became adept at working with these tools and

Catholic priest, was living in Michigan and had agreed to be our family's sponsor. We arrived as legal immigrants with Green Cards in hand. My parents enrolled my older twin brothers, Tom and Joy, in school, got them settled in, and took me back home to India with them. Every six months my dad would bring me back to America to make sure my Green Card didn't expire. My father's foresight and belief that his children should have a global perspective governed his commitment to our education and broadened our access to the world. Shortly after returning from one of these trips to the United States, my father died suddenly. The impact of his passing was profound; my mother and I were living

SPARKED BY MY ALWAYS CURIOUS APPETITE, I SET UPON AN ENTHUSIASTIC INVESTIGATION OF THE FOODS OF MY PROVINCE AND THE NEARBY CITIES OF THE MALABAR REGION, PARTICULARLY THE PORTS WITH THEIR HISTORIC CREOLE-LIKE BLENDING OF SPICES AND FLAVORS BROUGHT BY ARAB, ROMAN, PORTUGUESE, DUTCH, BRITISH, AND ASIAN TRADERS AND SETTLERS.

embraced the eclectic flavors that abound for those who live along the historical spice route.

Sparked by my always curious appetite, I set upon an enthusiastic investigation of the foods of my province and the nearby cities of the Malabar region, particularly the ports with their historic Creole-like blending of spices and flavors brought by Arab, Roman, Portuguese, Dutch, British, and Asian traders and settlers. I eagerly anticipated the Jewish, Christian, Muslim, and Hindu festivals and the myriad of enticing foods they featured throughout the year. Traveling with my family broadened my palate and fed my inquisitive streak as I sampled unaccustomed flavors and ingredients and witnessed new cooking techniques.

I first journeyed to the United States when I was thirteen years old. My uncle Benjamin Gomez, a

in India and my college-aged brothers were abroad. The worldliness that had been a benchmark of our family's success and adaptability now left us scattered and stunned. My twin brothers advised us to join them. So, my mother and I immigrated to the United States permanently. I called Queens, New York, home for fourteen years before I married and moved south to Georgia in 2000.

My mother started catering parties and banquets in Queens with me by her side as her inexperienced, and not particularly willing, teen apprentice. She cooked for the multicultural diaspora of New York City. She began to realize, as had so many other widowed mothers and newly arrived immigrants before her, that cooking for others was a way to move forward with her life. I now see this insight as a great gift from her.

Naturally, as a young woman in a big city full of choices, I wanted to find my own way and decided to pursue a career as an aesthetician. Here I was, a precocious high schooler, telling my family I wanted to go to beauty school . . . needless to say it was not well received. I am descended from a family deeply committed to education; they are engineers, doctors, and professors. "No way, no how" was the reaction of my higher-education-minded mother and brothers to the prospect of a family member becoming a "beauty school dropout," much like the character in the song from the musical *Grease.* My family insisted I attend a real college, so I enrolled in Queens College at age sixteen to study psychology. My college credits placated my family, but I did not abandon my aesthetician goal.

Determined to fashion a life on my own terms, I found work in some of New York City's finest spas. I developed an interest in ayurveda, an ancient Indian system of healing that originated in my home state. Ayurveda considers healing and prolonging life as a matter of balance between the senses and the influences within the body. I returned to India for a year and a half to study traditional ayurvedic treatments in the cities of Trivandrum and Bombay.

Back in New York and having fulfilled aesthetician-licensing requirements, I worked as a skin care consultant for Victoria's Secret models, taught a variety of classes, and participated in research and development studies with several pharmaceutical companies.

I met Bobby Palayam in 1998, and we married in 2000. We had agreed that adoption would be the route we would pursue to become parents. So, when the time seemed right, we started the adoption process through an agency here in the US to adopt our son from India. After thirteen months' wait, we joyfully traveled to India to meet our son, Ethan, a charming three-year-old, and bring him home. Ethan has been the singular most important, beautiful, and satisfying decision we have ever made in our lives. I love being Ethan's mom. He fulfills my life in ways I never knew possible.

My independent streak and entrepreneurial spirit drove me to open my own ayurvedic spa. After we relocated in Atlanta, I launched the luxurious Neem Tree Spa. In the business's early years, we lived in an apartment above the spa. At the end of clients' appointments, I would often go upstairs to my home kitchen and bring down a Keralan meal of vegetable *biryani* and *thoran* for all to share. Just as the balance of elements representing fire, earth, water, and wind promote a healthy body, a balanced presentation of flavors of hot, cool, spicy, savory, and sweet lends itself to a memorable meal. Clearly, something inside of me wanted to touch all the senses, including taste.

It's funny: it was like I was running a secret Indian restaurant hidden inside a spa. Folks had to get a facial or a massage to eat my food. These ayurvedic after-treatment parties nourished and awakened sensibilities and appetites in both my guests and myself.

The spa closed in 2008 after the steep economic downturn. I continued to correspond with many of my former patrons who lamented the loss of my rejuvenating treatments. Equally missed was the comfort found in the healthful plates of food offered at the end of spa appointments. This groundswell of support prompted me to host a supper club highlighting regional Keralan cuisine out of my home. The plan to hold one or two supper club dinners before I opened my next spa morphed into an every weekend event. Supper club dinners were selling out within minutes of being announced. I was forced to rent space in which I could cook for upward of two hundred guests. Diners enjoyed gentle coconut-based stews, spiced vegetable and yogurt salads, and goat *biryani*, as well as fish and seafood curries ranging from tangy to smoky, served with delectable sweet and savory breads made from rice flour batters. I chose descriptive themed names for my dishes, like Spice Route Fish Fry, to intrigue diners. The menus featured riffs on American southern favorites and quickly became known as "South by South dinners."

An understanding of port-city cooking can only evolve after one has lived and eaten in an area where the intermingling of foods and cooking techniques constantly changes as ships arrive and depart. I have lived in several great seaports—Thope and Mumbai in India and New York City—and witnessed firsthand the impact

ing for others. In a way, this profession of chef chose me. Cardamom Hill, my first foray into the restaurant business, opened in January 2012. Heady critical acclaim soon followed, and the business was a great success. But balancing the demands of a white-linen restaurant with motherhood led me to make some tough decisions. I knew I wanted to continue to cook professionally, but I also realized I wanted to be home with my son in the evenings, so I closed Cardamom Hill in July 2014. I had recently opened Third Space, a culinary event venue near my home. Third Space's open kitchen provided a

MY RECIPES ARE A MINGLING OF COOKING STYLES AND FLAVORS ROOTED IN MY AFFECTION FOR THESE TWO LOCALES, AND I FIND THIS JOURNEY ENDLESSLY EXCITING.

varied cultural exchanges can have on a population's eating habits. Atlanta enjoys its own complex cultural crosswind. My travels to the port cities of Savannah, Charleston, New Orleans, and Miami have spurred me to develop my own interpretation of some of their favorite local dishes. Along both the fabled Malabar Coast and the Gulf of Mexico's shores, spices and produce follow the seasons, the tides, and the manifests of the boats that come into their ports. All sorts of ingredients make their way into the larders and pantries of these regions, and certain foodstuffs might only be available for a fleeting period of time. Local cooks learn to work with ingenuity and a certain daring—a sensibility still at play here in the American South. My recipes are a mingling of cooking styles and flavors rooted in my affection for these two locales, and I find this journey endlessly exciting.

The enthusiastic support and encouragement of patrons, friends, and family helped me to recognize that by returning to my kitchen roots, my personal "spice route" had come full circle once again. Much like my mother, I moved my own life forward by cook-

place for me to teach cooking classes and was the perfect location to reinstate those intimate, private dinners and forums for my style of cooking. Not long afterward, our imprint expanded with the opening of Spice to Table in a space next door. The culinary conversation I had started with my adopted hometown could continue in these settings and allow a more balanced work and home life.

Now, my life is filled with the joys of being a mother, the daily challenges of being a business owner, and the gift of being able to work as a CARE chef ambassador.

When I'm cooking in my little Indian patisserie, Spice to Table, or teaching a class at Third Space and find myself in the company of a guest who says something tastes delicious, my immediate reaction is to share the recipe and tell the guest how easy it will be to replicate the dish in their kitchen. This book, I hope, will further the sharing of favorite dishes and the inquisitive exploration of flavors started by those early supper club evenings. I am pleased to share my personal journey through this album of recipes as a way to bring the flavors of my two Souths into kitchens everywhere.

# a few notes on ingredients

*Several of Kerala's unique ingredients are listed in recipes throughout this book. I thought it might be handy to talk a bit about these up front.*

The Keralan palate is drawn to sour, pungent, and camphoraceous flavors. In these recipes I cook with *kodampuli*, *asafoetida*, and curry leaves. For those familiar with these ingredients, I hope to share new ways to use them by incorporating them into favorite regional dishes. And for those trying these spices for the first time, your flavor vocabulary will certainly be enhanced with vibrant new tastes.

I am in the habit of calling finely ground spices *powder*. I think it makes them sound more magical, and frankly, I do feel they contain some mystical powers. Generally, I grind spices with a mortar and pestle. For larger batches or if a very fine powder is needed, I will use a small coffee grinder. For grating nutmeg and citrus zest, a Microplane grater works best.

My *masal dhabba*, the ubiquitous spice tin found in Indian kitchens, holds Kashmiri chili powder, green cardamom pods, turmeric, and garam masala, as well as mustard seeds, cumin seeds, cloves, and cinnamon sticks.

Unless otherwise specified, use the following glossary for reference and clarification of ingredients called for in this book's recipes.

### ◆ ALLSPICE

Sometimes referred to as *pimenta* (not to be confused with pimiento, the pepper), allspice is the sundried, cured unripe fruit of a tropical evergreen tree. Unprocessed, the berries look like swollen peppercorns. When powdered, the aroma of allspice is redolent of cinnamon, cloves, and nutmeg all combined together with strong citrus notes. When purchasing whole allspice, look for dried berries with a deep, dark reddish-brown color and rough surface with no hint of mustiness in the aroma. Powdered allspice should also have a deep brown color and rich aroma and possess a slightly oily—never dusty—feel when pinched.

### ◆ ASAFOETIDA

This seasoning is derived from a giant, ten-foot-tall cousin of fennel. The plants are tapped much like rubber plants, and the mastic is dried and ground into a powder. This flavoring is sold in amounts called tears, blocks, and pieces but is more commonly found in powdered form, which is the dried resin ground with a starch to make it more manageable. Also known as stinking gum, *hing*, or devil's dung, the uncooked spice has a strong fetid smell, so a well-sealed container is needed to keep it from permeating the entire spice cabinet.

However, once cooked, asafoetida provides a smooth flavor reminiscent of leeks. For people who follow the Jain faith and are prohibited from eating garlic, asafoetida is often used in its place.

### ◆ BUTTER

I like to use unsalted European-style butters. They are churned more slowly and have less water, or whey, than many widely distributed American brands. These high-quality butters have a fat content between 83 and 86 percent. The most widely distributed American brands' fat content is around 80 percent. Having a higher fat content will make clarified butter, ghee, and *beurre noisette* richer with a slightly higher yield. Techniques for making each of these butter variations are described within the recipes. My favorite brands of ghee are Amul and Deep. Whole Foods carries a great brand called Organic India.

Clarified butter and ghee are quite similar. The only difference is

that in making ghee the milk solids are allowed to lightly caramelize, lending a slightly nutty flavor to the pure butterfat before it is strained away.

To make ghee, heat unsalted butter in a heavy-bottomed pot over low heat until melted. Let the butter simmer until the foam rises to the top. The butter will then sputter. Once the sputtering stops, no more foam is rising to the top, and the milk solids in the bottom have turned a khaki color, remove it from the heat. Skim any foam off the top with a spoon. Strain the remaining butter into a container, taking care to leave behind any solids in the pot. Ghee will keep in the refrigerator for up to six months.

### ◆ CANE SYRUP

This syrup is made from sugarcane stalks, which are crushed to extrude the juice. It is extremely sweet, with a medium viscosity, much like maple syrup (molasses is also made from cane sugar but is further processed into a thick, dark product). In the American South, I often see cane syrup used on pancakes, biscuits, and waffles, and it is frequently sold at roadside stands.

### ◆ CARDAMOM

I mostly use green cardamom, though a few of the recipes in this book call for the black variety. I crush the pods of either variety before using them in a recipe. The true flavor of cardamom is contained in the seeds inside the pod. Crush the pods with a mortar and pestle to break them open and release these seeds. These crushed pods contribute cardamom's robust flavor to a finished dish. The other way I use cardamom is to grind the seeds to a fine powder in a spice blender or coffee grinder. Green cardamom is a member of the ginger family, is indigenous to Sri Lanka and southern India, and has a faintly eucalyptus-like bouquet. It is the third-most expensive spice in the world—eclipsed only by saffron and vanilla—only a small amount is needed to impart cardamom's full flavor. Try to purchase the pods, as once the spice is ground it tends to lose flavor. However, if pods are unavailable, ground cardamom will work. Generally, ten pods are equivalent to 1½ teaspoons of ground cardamom.

Look for closed pods of black cardamom (also known as brown or Nepal cardamom) in glass containers or bags in the spice aisle of your grocery or at specialty stores. The pods may look flaky, but that is fine as long as they are not broken or split. The seeds inside the pods are sticky with a tar-like resin and lose potency once the pods are split. When first harvested in mountainous areas, these pods are bright red, but the pods are dried over low-burning fires, which turn them a dark brownish black and impart a smoky flavor. Chinese or Thai brown cardamom is usually sundried, resulting in a more camphoric, less smoky flavor.

### ◆ CLOVES

Look for whole cloves with the small friable ball still attached to the nail-like stem. When purchasing ground cloves, look for a powder with a dark brown color and strong aroma; lighter colored and fibrous powders are most likely cut with a good bit of clove stem and will not deliver the same robust flavor.

### ◆ COCONUT

Honestly, I rarely crack and shred a whole coconut. Very high-quality, shredded, fresh unsweetened coconut is available frozen at many groceries and can likely be found in the freezer section of Indian, Latin, and Asian markets. When I use frozen coconut, I like Keralan coconut sold under the Laxmi brand.

**Dried, unsweetened, flaked.** Dried unsweetened coconut, also called *copra* or desiccated coconut, can be found in the baking or health-food sections of most markets. Bob's Red Mill Unsweetened Flaked Coconut is a widely available quality brand; it is not pristinely white because it is not processed with sulfides, which are used to retain the whiteness. In a pinch, reconstitute the dried coconut by soaking it in very hot water for twenty minutes, then lightly squeeze out the water and use in place of fresh or frozen grated coconut.

**Dried, sweetened.** Dried sweetened coconut is moistened by an infusion of sugar and used mostly in baking and desserts and is sold in bags or cans in the baking aisle.

### ◆ COCONUT MILK

I find Chaokoh Coconut Milk in the brown and white can works perfectly. Remember to always give the can a good shake before using the milk. Coconut milk is extracted from the white meat of a coconut. It is made by simmering the fresh meat with water and then the mixture is pressed to extract the liquid. Do not use sweetened cream of coconut in these recipes; save that for cocktails.

### ◆ COCONUT OIL

This oil is derived from pressing dried coconut meat. The two main types available to the home cook are refined and unrefined. Refined Parachute coconut oil, which comes in a bright blue bottle, is the brand I use most often in my kitchen. Be sure to purchase 100 percent pure coconut oil for cooking (some coconut oil products used for cosmetic purposes may contain mineral oil).

### ◆ CURRY LEAVES

These small, vivid green, spade-shaped leaves lend their citrusy, spicy, mouth-watering acerbity to curry dishes and seafood stews. The name comes from its use as opposed to its flavor. This plant, which is grown in most Keralan home gardens, is a relative of citrus, though it produces no fruits, and has a flavor that Keralans adore. Most often, curry leaves are fried in hot oil at the beginning of a dish's preparation to extract their biting flavor and are also used in marinades. These fresh leaves will keep refrigerated in a resealable plastic bag for about a week. Dried curry leaves are available and can be used, though the dish will lack some brightness.

### ◆ FENUGREEK

A member of the legume family, this plant is used as an herb (leaves), spice (seeds), and vegetable (leaves, sprouts, and microgreens). The light khaki seeds measure about $1/16$ of an inch and are cuboid shaped with an indention on one side. Since the seeds resemble bits of gravel and the plant grows near the sea in sandy tracts and dry riverbeds, fenugreek seeds should be combed through before using to make sure no tiny bits of grit are mixed in. Bitter uncooked, once toasted the seeds lend a slightly maple, burnt-caramel flavor to dishes.

### ◆ GARAM MASALA

The word *masala* simply means a blend of spices. Garam masala is a distinctive blend of spices that vary from region to region or from cook to cook. Look for this blend in Indian or other specialty spice stores. You can also make your own by blending 4 teaspoons ground fennel seeds, $2^{1/2}$ teaspoons each of ground cinnamon and ground caraway, and $1/2$ teaspoon each of ground black peppercorns, ground cloves, and ground green cardamom seeds. Note that the blend called for in this recipe does *not* contain cumin and coriander, commonly found in many "curry-style" powders.

### ◆ JAGGERY

Jaggery is much more than a mere sweetener in cooking. A type of sugar, jaggery also plays a healing and spiritual role in ayurvedic practices and is thought to bring good luck if a few bites are eaten before commencing a new venture.

This deep amber to brown sweetener is an unrefined sugar made from sugarcane juice that has been reduced and set into blocks for molding into loaves. Any time my mother wanted to sweeten something, she'd shave off a bit from the jaggery loaf that sat wrapped in a burlap bag on her kitchen counter and melt it down to use in a recipe. Here in the States, I can find it at most Indian markets. I absolutely adore its deep, somewhat winey flavor. Jaggery can also be made from date palm and toddy palm; I prefer it made from sugarcane.

### ◆ KASHMIRI CHILI POWDER

This mildly hot, vibrantly vermillion powder is used to both color and flavor dishes. Kashmiri chili powder is pleasingly sweet with a pronounced bite. Though hot paprika can be substituted in a pinch, this deep crimson powder lends a special flavor and is worth seeking out. A quick online search will result in multiple sources for delivery of this exotic seasoning to your front door.

### ◆ KODAMPULI

This spice is sometimes called *gambodge* or the misnomer Malabar tamarind (since it is no relation to tamarind); it is derived from a small, yellow fruit looking much like a tiny pumpkin. The tangy fruit is picked, seeded, sundried, smoked until black, and then rubbed with a mixture of oil and salt before being tightly sealed in earthenware vessels. The smokey, sour, somewhat puckery flavor is loved across coastal India. It's considered essential to a proper fish curry and cannot easily be substituted. I have found that once folks in the US try *kodampuli*, they will seek out dishes with it. It is considered a "gateway flavor" for anyone interested in Keralan cuisine. It can be purchased at specialty and Indian groceries and online and has an indefinite shelf life. If you can't get your hands on *kodampuli*, substitute 1 tablespoon tamarind paste—but I assure you it is worth tracking down. The dried fruit pieces look like a small, hollow black log. Once rehydrated, it has a leathery feel and looks like small pieces of dark-brown pumpkin rind.

### ◆ MUSTARD SEEDS

The recipes in this book often call for brown mustard seeds. However, when I want a more pungent, mustardy flavor and a pronounced bite, I opt for black mustard seeds. Brown seeds have about 70 percent of the pungency of black seeds.

Black mustard seeds are specifically derived from the plant *Brassica nigra*. These round, hard seeds vary in color, from dark brown to black. They are tricky to harvest because the seedpods shatter easily, accounting for their higher price. The scent, pop, and crackle of dark mustard seeds as they hit hot oil is an aroma and sound you will grow to love in your kitchen.

### ◆ RICE

In my kitchen I primarily prepare basmati rice. "Queen of Fragrance" is a frequent translation of the word *basmati*. To obtain a dry, fluffy texture, bring the rice and water to a boil and then cook the rice covered on low heat for 10 minutes. Remove the pot from the heat. Leave the lid on the pot for 7 minutes. The residual heat will continue to steam the rice, and the excess moisture. Uncover and fluff the rice with a fork.

### ◆ STAR ANISE

The fruit of a member of the magnolia family, *Illicium verum* is native to northeast Vietnam and southeast China. Star anise is botanically unrelated to the herb anise, but it nevertheless contains the same essential oil that gives both plants a nearly identical strong, sweet licorice flavor. Many liqueurs with an anise or licorice flavor are actually made with an extract of star anise.

### ◆ TAMARIND

Even though tamarind is now grown commercially in southern regions of the United States where its worldwide production is second only to India, fresh tamarind can still be hard to find. Even if you can locate fresh pods, you must carefully peel and seed it and remove the fiber before using the pulp. Tamarind pulp can also be purchased in blocks, but the concentrates that I suggest using in these recipes are readily available. I like a concentrate brand called Tamicon. Bear in mind that the concentrates tend to be a tad more sour than sweet. Tamarind has a good deal of tartaric acid, making it a favorite agent for sour—a flavor for which we coastal Indians are so fond.

### ◆ TURMERIC

This golden-hued spice has been valued through the ages for its medicinal use as well as in beauty treatments and rituals. When I was little and had a minor cut or bruise, my mom would put turmeric powder on the cut before she put a bandage on it. I do the same for my son, Ethan, trusting in the anti-inflammatory and antimicrobial qualities of curcumin, a substance found in this healing spice. It is also used in many beauty treatments and rituals throughout India. Often the day before a wedding, a bride's body is covered in a paste of fresh sandalwood and turmeric as a symbolic rite of purity, fertility, and auspicious beginnings.

Turmeric is ground from the dried rhizome of a tropical perennial that looks like ginger with a rounder shape and a deep orangey-yellow-colored center. Quality ground turmeric powder will have an earthy aroma and a bitter, lingering flavor with an ever-so-light oily feel to the powder. Work cautiously with turmeric—it leaves stains that can be almost impossible to remove. If you do stain white clothing or table linens, try soaking the item in a plastic container for about an hour with 2 tablespoons of granular sodium perborate (denture cleaner) dissolved in 1 quart cool water; rinse and launder with bleach. Let the laundered cloth dry in bright sunlight to oxidize the stain.

# CHAPTER ONE
## day starters

*My mornings start around 5:30 a.m. with a cup of black Assam tea, a quick look at my e-mails, and a quiet moment to myself.*

Soon, my precious Kira Girl, my frail fifteen-year-old King Charles spaniel, comes padding up to spend some time with me before I wake my child and get his day started. On weekdays, it's a bit rushed in the mornings getting Ethan ready for school, so I make a quick breakfast bowl of grits or an egg *appam*. An egg *appam* only takes a few minutes to cook once the batter is ready. Sometimes he just opts for a bowl of cereal, or we both grab smoothies as we scoot out the door. After dropping Ethan off at school, I can get my workday started.

Many mornings begin with me cruising through one of our local farmers' markets. The DeKalb Farmers Market is a favorite for fresh traditional Georgia crops, and the Buford Highway Farmers Market offers the wares of a collection of small farmers providing the produce of their homelands far from the shelves of megamarkets. On weekends, the Peachtree Road Farmers Market, where many of the local specialty farmers gather, is a joyous neighborly affair. A couple of times a month, I visit the Burundi Women's Farm, a co-op affiliated with the Global Growers Association. Some of these women dress in the traditional Burundi *pagne*, a wraparound garment of colorful geometric prints, and wear remarkable, intricately tied headdresses. They farm a swath of land across from a metro station, with trains and busses arriving and departing. It is a sight to behold! I get a real charge out of living in this city of Atlanta and seeing a world of flavors and folks all around me.

Once the marketing is done, I stop by a favorite neighborhood café, Octane, for a much-needed cup of coffee. Refreshed, I head for my office at Spice to Table. My staff and I look through the finds from my farmers' market runs and peruse the bounty our friends, farmers, and purveyors bring our way to decide what will be showcased on the day's menu. We end this collaborative time filled with inspiration, motivation, and excitement to create delicious offerings for our guests. With my pantry full, the day's cooking begins.

Weekends are more laid back, with Saturday mornings starting later than our weekday routine. Ethan often joins me at Spice to Table or Third Space, working as a scene booster and DJ. He keeps the tunes flowing for diners and kitchen crew alike with his singular mix of Led Zeppelin, Bollywood, and a bit of Lynyrd Skynyrd thrown in to keep the vibe going.

With the restaurant closed on Sundays, Ethan, his dad, Bobby, and I enjoy cooking together at home, preparing a family breakfast feast. We three agree it is our favorite day of the week. Sometimes we find ourselves inviting a houseful of friends of all ages for a fun-filled brunch. We really love making an elaborate breakfast or brunch for our friends and neighbors. I do adore an all-day brunch!

# egg appam

AN *APPAM* IS A BOWL-SHAPED, fermented rice-flour crêpe made with coconut milk. It has a spongy, cake-like bottom and lacy crisp edges and is often featured as a breakfast item or served alongside stews. The batter keeps for a week in the refrigerator, so a single batch can yield several mornings' worth of breakfasts. Kerala's lush green landscape includes swaying coconut palms and curving, undulating rice paddies. These two familiar crops are essential sources of income and provide the necessary ingredients for this common, yet elegant, dish. It is traditionally cooked in a two-handled, round-sided, shallow bowl-shaped pan called an *appachatti*, which is commercially available in cast-iron or nonstick metal varieties.

For this recipe, I prefer a larger, open version of the *appachatti* pan, but any deep, rounded pan with a cover will suffice. My mother made these frilly-edged crêpe bowls for our family many mornings at our Carmel Compound home. The early morning sounds of ladies chattering amid the clatter of pots and pans in the kitchens and the clamor of fishermen pulling their nets in the salty sea air mixed deliciously with the *appam*'s yeasty aroma to welcome the day. The softly set egg centered in this delicate crêpe reminds me of sunrises along the beaches I roamed as a child.

# EGG APPAM

2 tablespoons semolina flour

1 tablespoon plus 1 teaspoon white granulated sugar

1/2 teaspoon active dry yeast

2 cups white rice flour

2 cups coconut milk

1/4 teaspoon kosher salt plus a pinch for the egg yolk

8 large eggs

In a 2-quart saucepan, combine 2 cups of water and the semolina. Cook over medium heat, stirring occasionally, until the semolina has the consistency of porridge and the water is absorbed, 3 to 5 minutes.

In a small bowl, mix 1 cup warm water with 1 teaspoon of the sugar. Sprinkle the yeast over the water and allow to proof until foamy, about 15 minutes.

In a 4-quart bowl, combine the rice flour, cooked semolina, yeast mixture, and 2 cups of the coconut milk. Stir the batter until it is well combined. Cover and let sit at room temperature for at least 3 hours to ferment. Batter can ferment overnight or up to 8 hours.

When ready to cook the *appam*, stir the batter thoroughly. Add the tablespoon of sugar and the teaspoon of salt and stir. If the batter seems too thick stir in water 1 tablespoon at a time until the batter has the consistency of a pancake batter.

Spray an *appachatti* pan or any rounded pan with oil. Heat the pan over medium heat. Ladle 5 to 6 tablespoons of the batter into the pan and rotate the pan to coat the bottom; form a shallow bowl slightly thicker at the bottom and thinning toward the top edge. Cook for 1 minute. Crack an egg into the center of the batter. Cover and let cook until the egg is just set and the edges are slightly brown, about 3 minutes. Sprinkle the remaining pinch of salt on the egg yolk. Using a spatula, gently remove the egg appam from the pan. Repeat with the remaining batter and eggs. Serve warm or hot.

**NOTES:** *This batter may be stored covered in the refrigerator for up to one week. Stir the batter thoroughly before using after refrigeration.*

# spice to table date oatmeal

THIS IS BREAKFAST CEREAL GONE GLOBAL. Steel-cut Irish oatmeal is cooked in coconut milk, seasoned with Indian spices bloomed in butter, and graced with North African Medjool dates. This seems a fitting dish for Atlanta, the truly international city I now call home. One of my Saturday morning routines is to head out to a Middle Eastern market, Shahrzad, in Roswell on the outskirts of Atlanta to buy spices, Medjool dates, and nuts. Ethan loves to come along on these visits as he finds them to be mini international field trips. Medjool dates, prized for their large, juicy sweetness, are an excellent source of fiber, B vitamins, and potassium. Look for dried dates that are plump with no spots. They are often more expensive but offer the richest flavor.

**MAKES 4 SERVINGS**

1 tablespoon ghee

6 green cardamom pods, crushed

1/2 teaspoon turmeric powder

1 1/2 cups steel-cut Irish oats, toasted (see notes)

1 tablespoon packed light-brown sugar

1 teaspoon kosher salt

1 1/2 cups coconut milk

1/2 cup thinly sliced pitted Medjool dates

Heat a 2-quart saucepan over medium heat. Add the ghee, the cardamom, and the turmeric. Cook and stir for 30 seconds. Add 2 1/2 cups of water and the oats and bring to a boil. Add the brown sugar and salt, reduce the heat to low, and cook for 20 minutes, stirring occasionally.

Add the coconut milk and cook until the liquid is absorbed and the oatmeal is creamy, about 10 minutes. Sprinkle the dates over each serving of oatmeal.

**NOTES**: *To toast the oatmeal, bake it at 375°F for 5 to 7 minutes or until light golden brown. This adds a unique nutty, toasty flavor to the oats and makes them a perfect match for the sweet Medjool dates.*

*Steel-cut oatmeal is simply whole oat groats—husked, whole grain, which includes the cereal grain as well as the fiber-rich bran portion—that have been cut into tiny pieces, as opposed to the more common rolled oats found in the United States. McCann's Irish Oatmeal is a widely available brand and comes in a cool-looking, classic metal tin for storage.*

# nutmeg scented crêpes *filled with* coconut *and* jaggery

GROWING UP, *CHURLLAPPAM*, or "curled bread," was the name I knew for what are more widely known as crêpes. In this recipe, sweet little fragments of shaved jaggery intermingle with strands of fresh coconut and gratings of sweet-smelling nutmeg, which are swaddled in tender crêpe parcels.

1 cup frozen, grated fresh coconut, thawed

1/4 cup shaved jaggery

1 teaspoon freshly grated nutmeg, divided

3/4 cup whole milk

1 large egg

4 teaspoons melted ghee, divided

1/2 cup unbleached all-purpose flour

1/2 cup cane syrup

Additional nutmeg for dusting, if desired

**MAKES 8 CRÊPES, 4 SERVINGS**

In a small bowl, combine the coconut, shaved jaggery, and 1/2 teaspoon of the nutmeg and set aside while preparing the crêpes.

In a medium bowl, whisk together the milk, egg, 2 teaspoons of the ghee, flour, and the remaining 1/2 teaspoon of nutmeg. The mixture will be the consistency of a thin, lump-free pancake batter.

Heat an 8-inch nonstick skillet over medium heat. Add 1/4 teaspoon of ghee to the pan and swirl to coat the pan. Ladle 2 tablespoons of batter into the center of the pan and swirl to spread the batter evenly to ensure a very thin crêpe.

Cook each crêpe for 30 seconds, and then flip the crêpe over. Place 2 teaspoons of the coconut mixture in the center of the crêpe and fold in each side, as if folding a letter, then remove from pan. Repeat with the remaining batter and filling.

Drizzle finished crêpes with cane syrup and dust with nutmeg, if desired.

# egg bhurji

WHEN I WAS IN THE TENTH GRADE, my cousin Johnny left our compound to go to medical school in Bangalore, India. After getting settled, he invited me to visit him. He lived in an apartment with a few roommates close to campus. The first morning I was there, I woke up to my cousin telling me he was going to make *bhurji* for breakfast and just how very delicious it would be. I had no clue what he was talking about. The term was not something with which I was familiar. Lo and behold, egg *bhurji*—or, as it is sometimes called, *anda bhurji*—basically turned out to be scrambled eggs with shallots, chiles, tomatoes, herbs, and spices. It is a very common street food throughout India. I don't know why I did not recognize its "official" name; though, in my defense, it is known by different names in different regions. India has twenty-two different languages and hundreds of different dialects. No wonder this name for dressed-up scrambled eggs had escaped me. I remember having a good laugh when I realized that all he was doing was making me scrambled eggs. But his take on the dish turned out to be so much more. The added spices and fresh ingredients took his egg *bhurji* to a whole other level. To this day when I make *bhurji* in the morning at home, I find myself smiling at the memory of discovering the name of this incredible version of simple scrambled eggs.

8 large eggs

2 tablespoons whole milk

1 tablespoon canola oil

1 medium shallot, finely chopped

1 jalapeño, seeded and finely chopped

1 medium Roma tomato, seeded and finely chopped

2 tablespoons finely chopped cilantro leaves

1/4 teaspoon crushed red pepper flakes

1/4 teaspoon kosher salt

Crack the eggs into a medium bowl, add the milk, whisk together, and set aside.

In a medium skillet over medium heat, cook the shallots in the canola oil until they are translucent, about 1 minute. Add the jalapeño, tomatoes, cilantro, red pepper flakes, and salt and cook for 2 to 3 minutes, stirring occasionally, until the juices of the tomatoes evaporate. Turning the heat to low, add the eggs and fold in the ingredients gently, stirring until the mixture curdles, about 1 minute. Increase the heat to high then vigorously stir the mixture, taking care to break up any large lumps and scraping the sides of the pan. Cook until the scrambled eggs are no longer runny, about 30 seconds. Serve warm.

# skillet chicken hash pie

VARIATIONS OF SAVORY MEAT pies are found throughout the world. When I moved to the American South, I discovered there were numerous regional versions of meat pies there as well, each one sporting its unique twists with ingredients and presentation. In this recipe, I have combined elements to create a tribute to these mouthwatering provincial favorites. Garam masala and turmeric pay homage to Kerala, while the cream cheese crust adds a southern tenderness. Both the dough and filling for this hearty breakfast pie can be prepared the night before and then assembled and baked in the morning.

## CREAM CHEESE PIECRUST

3 cups unbleached all-purpose flour

1 1/2 teaspoons kosher salt

1/2 teaspoon baking powder

18 tablespoons (2 sticks plus 2 tablespoons) unsalted butter, chilled and cut into small pieces

7 ounces (just under one 8-ounce block) cream cheese, chilled and cut into small pieces

1/4 cup very cold water

**MAKES TWO 9-INCH PIE CRUSTS, 2.6 POUNDS OF DOUGH**

In the bowl of an electric mixer, combine the flour, salt, and baking powder. With the mixer running at low speed, add the butter a few pieces at a time, mixing until the butter is in small pea-sized pieces. Add the cream cheese and mix until the cream cheese gets incorporated and starts forming a shaggy dough. Gradually drizzle the cold water over the dough and mix until the dough clears the side of the bowl. Form the dough into 2 flat disks; wrap the dough in plastic wrap and chill for at least 1 hour or up 2 days. Roll the dough into two 1/4-inch-thick and 10-inch-round circles.

**NOTES:** *Take this advice: when making piecrust, prepare two and freeze one! With a homemade piecrust in the freezer, whipping up a tasty treat for drop-in company or an effortless brunch on a lazy Sunday will be a snap. Roll the extra crust up between two pieces of waxed or parchment paper, and slip it into a freezer bag. I store mine in the freezer door where it is less likely to get smashed or lost among the shelves.*

## HASH FILLING

2 tablespoons canola oil

1 large yellow onion, thinly sliced

1 teaspoon peeled, finely chopped
fresh ginger

3 garlic cloves, finely chopped

1 teaspoon garam masala

1/2 teaspoon turmeric powder

11/2 teaspoons kosher salt

2 teaspoons tomato paste

1 pound cooked chicken breast, cut
into bite-sized pieces

1 cup fresh or frozen green peas

2 small gold potatoes, peeled, boiled,
and smashed to pieces or roughly
chopped

5 large eggs, beaten

1/2 teaspoon crushed red pepper
flakes, for garnish

1/2 teaspoon dried parsley flakes,
for garnish

Line a 10-inch cast-iron skillet with one circle of the dough. Place the dough in the skillet and chill in the refrigerator while preparing the filling. (Reserve the other crust for future use.)

In another large skillet, heat the oil over medium heat. Add the onions and ginger and cook until the onions are golden brown, 5 to 6 minutes. Add the garlic, cooking and stirring for 2 minutes. Add the garam masala, turmeric powder, and salt, cooking and stirring for an additional 1 minute.

Add the tomato paste and 1/2 cup of water, stirring well to fully incorporate all the ingredients. Add the chicken and continue to cook, stirring occasionally until all of the liquid evaporates. Add the peas and potatoes and stir well to combine. Cook, stirring occasionally, until everything is coated and well combined, for 2 to 3 minutes. Remove from the heat and cool.

Heat the oven to 350°F.

Stir the hash filling into the eggs. Pour the mixture into the prepared crust and bake until the top is a light golden brown, approximately 25 minutes. Garnish with a sprinkling of red pepper flakes and dried parsley flakes. Cool for 15 minutes and serve it right out of the skillet.

**NOTES:** *This pastry dough is quite forgiving and, consequently, my favorite. Some folks are intimidated by the idea of making pastry dough. This cream cheese piecrust has a bit of baking powder, which yields extra flakiness, and cream cheese, which ensures tenderness. I'm sure you will adore working with this dough. But I'm a working mom and understand that if you want, or need, to whip out a refrigerated crust from the market, do what you've got to do.*

# blueberry lime muffins

I ALWAYS HAVE FRESH LIMES IN THE KITCHEN. For this delightful day starter, I have added the delicate spice mace. Mace is an underused seasoning. It is made from the brittle, ruddy-orange web-like coating on the outside of a whole nutmeg seed. Mace is often relegated to pumpkin spice—quite a shame, considering how wonderfully it flavors fresh fruit.

**MAKES 12 MUFFINS**

## CRUMB TOPPING

1¼ cups unbleached all-purpose flour

½ cup packed light-brown sugar

½ teaspoon kosher salt

½ teaspoon cinnamon powder

½ teaspoon mace powder

8 tablespoons (1 stick) unsalted butter, melted and cooled

## MUFFINS

3 cups plus 2 tablespoons unbleached all-purpose flour

1 tablespoon baking powder

1 teaspoon kosher salt

6 tablespoons (¾ stick) unsalted butter plus 2 tablespoons for greasing tins, softened

1¼ cups white granulated sugar

1 teaspoon lime zest

1 large whole egg plus 2 large egg yolks

1 teaspoon pure vanilla extract

1 cup whole milk

2 cups fresh or frozen blueberries

For the crumb topping, in a medium bowl, whisk together the flour, brown sugar, salt, cinnamon, and mace. Drizzle the butter over the dry ingredients and mix with a fork to make a crumbly topping. Set aside.

For the muffins, heat oven to 375°F. Line a standard 12-cup muffin pan with paper liners. In another bowl, whisk together the flour, baking powder, and salt.

In the large bowl of an electric mixer set on medium speed, cream the butter, granulated sugar, and lime zest until fluffy, about 3 minutes. Add the eggs and vanilla; mix until well combined. Reduce speed to low; alternate adding reserved flour mixture and milk, beginning and ending with flour. Gently fold in the blueberries.

Divide the batter evenly among the muffin pan cups. Sprinkle the crumb topping evenly over the batter in each cup, and press the crumbs lightly into the batter with your fingers.

Bake until the crumbs on top are deep golden brown and the muffins spring back lightly when touched, about 20 minutes. Cool the muffins in the pan on a cooling rack for 5 minutes before turning them out. Serve warm or at room temperature.

# puffy ginger hoecakes

THE SPIRITED ZING OF FRESH GINGER ENLIVENS MY PUFFED VERSION of country-style fried cornmeal cakes, which southerners call hoecakes.

Although I grew up eating *uttappam*, a rice pancake seasoned with shallots, ginger, and chiles, I had never encountered homemade cornmeal hoecakes until I was having brunch at a friend's home here in Georgia. Her crispy hoecakes reminded me not only of Indian *uttappam* but also of Venezuelan *arepas*. Like many of the traditional dishes here in America's southern states, my friend's hoecakes evoked memories of my *other* South in India. So, the next morning, I couldn't wait to replicate them with some of the same ingredients used in an Indian *uttappam*. The resulting puffy ginger cakes have become a favorite breakfast and brunch menu item both at work and at home. I like to serve these crispy cornmeal cakes in the morning with Spicy Syrup (page 69).

**MAKES SIX 2-INCH CAKES**

1 cup self-rising flour

1 cup yellow self-rising cornmeal

2 large eggs

1¼ cups buttermilk

2 teaspoons white granulated sugar

1 teaspoon kosher salt

2 teaspoons peeled, finely chopped fresh ginger

2 green onions, white and green parts, thinly sliced

2 cups canola oil

In a large bowl, combine all ingredients except for the oil, stirring thoroughly and making sure to scrape the sides and bottom of the bowl to mix uniformly.

Heat the canola oil in a medium-sized skillet over medium heat. Drop the batter, about 2 tablespoons at a time, into the hot oil. Fry each hoecake until golden brown, about 2 to 3 minutes per side, flipping once with a spatula. Using a slotted spoon, remove each hoecake and drain in a single layer on a paper-towel-lined plate. Serve warm.

**NOTES:** *Self-rising flour and cornmeal already include salt and baking powder. To make 1 cup of your own self-rising cornmeal, mix ¾ cup plus 3 tablespoons of cornmeal with 1 tablespoon baking powder and ½ teaspoon salt. To make 1 cup of self-rising flour, mix ¾ cup plus 3 tablespoons all-purpose flour with 1½ teaspoons of baking powder and ½ teaspoon of salt.*

*To keep the cakes warm and crisp, keep them under an upside-down colander until ready to serve. The hoecakes will stay warm and crispy because the steam escapes through the holes!*

# golden kichadi grits

THIS IS ONE OF MY FAVORITE SOUTH BY SOUTH DISHES!
It blends elements from my two Souths into a lovely ginger- and
leek-seasoned combination of golden lentils and stone-ground
grits. Inspired by *kichadi*—a rice, lentil, and butter comfort food
found throughout India—it can be prepared humbly with only a
little spice, or made rich with a variety of added spices. Cooks in
the northern region of India were the first to elevate this simple
dish from a peasant food to one cooked and presented in royal
palaces. In this recipe, I took the liberty of substituting grits for
the rice and discovered that lentils and grits marry marvelously.
My always hungry son loves these elevated grits for breakfast.
With a belly full of this hearty porridge, I know Ethan will be
ready and able to face the trials of elementary school.

2 tablespoons unsalted butter

1 tablespoon peeled, finely chopped fresh ginger

2 leeks, thinly sliced and rinsed

3 cups whole milk

1 teaspoon kosher salt

1 teaspoon turmeric powder

3/4 cup coarse, stone-ground yellow grits (I like Anson Mills Antebellum Coarse Yellow Grits)

1/4 cup dried yellow lentils

In a 4-quart saucepan, melt the butter over medium heat. Add the ginger and the leeks. Cook and stir until the ginger is golden brown and the leeks are tender, about 3 minutes.

Add 3 cups of water, the milk, the salt, and the turmeric. Increase the heat and bring the mixture to a boil. Whisk in the grits. Cook the grits, stirring frequently and taking care not to scald the bottom, until creamy and tender, about 1½ hours. If the grits absorb all of the water and milk before they are done, add a little hot water as needed to thin them out until they reach the desired consistency.

Meanwhile, cook the lentils. In a small saucepan, combine 1½ cups water and lentils. Cook over medium heat until the lentils are tender, about 20 minutes. Set aside until the grits are ready.

Fold the cooked lentils into the grits and cook for an additional 3 minutes. Serve hot with a dollop of extra butter, if desired.

## SLOW COOKER METHOD

4 tablespoons (½ stick) unsalted butter

1 tablespoon peeled, finely chopped fresh ginger

2 medium leeks (about ½ pound), thinly sliced and rinsed

2 cups whole milk

1½ teaspoons kosher salt

1 teaspoon turmeric powder

1½ cups stone-ground grits

6 ounces cooked yellow lentils (see Golden Kichadi Grits directions)

In a 4-quart saucepan, melt the butter over medium heat. Add the ginger and the leeks. Cook and stir until the ginger is golden brown and the leeks are tender, about 3 minutes.

In a 3-quart slow cooker, combine 2 cups of water, the milk, salt, and turmeric and add the browned leeks and ginger.

Whisk in the grits; cover and cook on a high setting for 2½ to 3 hours, stirring every 45 minutes. Grits are ready when they are creamy and tender throughout. Fold in the yellow lentils and cook for another 3 minutes. Serve hot.

# cardamom stewed plantains

IF THERE IS ANY DISH that instantly ferries me back to my dearest childhood memories, it is this one. Whenever I was in the doldrums or feeling poorly, my mother would whip up this consoling, quick-to-make stew of coconut milk and sweet plantains. The cardamom seemed to act as a balm for whatever ailed me. And it still does today. As a mother, I have learned that this dish helps heal hurt feelings as well as tummy aches.

8 to 10 green cardamom pods, crushed

1/2 teaspoon kosher salt

3/4 cup white granulated sugar

4 ripe sweet plantains, peeled, cut into 1/2-inch rounds

2 cups coconut milk

In a 4-quart saucepan, bring 3 cups of water, the cardamom, the salt, and the sugar to a boil. Add the plantains and cook over medium heat until the plantains are fork tender, about 15 minutes. Add the coconut milk and bring just to a simmer. The stewed plantains will have the consistency of a chowder. Remove from heat. Serve warm or at room temperature.

**NOTES:** *To select ripe plantains in the market, look for those with very brown, mottled skin.*

# quick tellicherry buttermilk biscuits

IN KERALA, THE NATIVE BLACK PEPPER HARVEST COMES TO MARKET in late February each year. Although Tellicherry was the name of a fort the British East India Company manned off the Malabar Coast, the designation *Tellicherry* refers to the size of the peppercorn not the location of where the pepper vine grows. Peppercorns bigger than 4.25 mm are given this name, while those 4.75 mm and larger are called Tellicherry special extra bold. The boldness comes not from heat but from an alluring citrus-like character derived from leaving them on the vine longer. As the peppercorns grow larger, they lose some of their heat but develop more aroma. These are considered the best peppercorns in the world. The addition of my homeland's national spice to a tender buttermilk biscuit warms my heart as well as my taste buds. The simple fact that these biscuits come together so quickly might have you underestimating the complex flavor of the black pepper and the buttermilk. Just because they are fast and easy doesn't mean they aren't complex. The biscuit dough can be made 30 minutes before baking, if you like. Do not let the dough sit for more than 30 minutes as it will become bitter and will not rise.

These Tellicherry pepper–spiked biscuits are wonderful slathered with Tomato Clove Preserves (page 52). Split and filled with Egg Bhurji (page 36), these biscuits make a wildly flavorful breakfast sandwich.

## QUICK TELLICHERRY BUTTERMILK BISCUITS

4 tablespoons (½ stick) unsalted butter, chilled and cut into small pieces, plus 2 tablespoons melted

2 cups self-rising flour, sifted

2 teaspoons fresh coarsely ground black Tellicherry peppercorns

3/4 cup buttermilk

2 teaspoons unbleached all-purpose flour, for forming the biscuits

Pinch of kosher salt

Heat the oven to 450°F. Grease a 9-inch cast-iron skillet.

Using your fingertips or a pastry blender, mix the butter into the self-rising flour until it feels crumbly. Sprinkle the pepper over the flour mixture. Add the buttermilk and mix with a fork until a shaggy dough is formed. Dust your work surface with the all-purpose flour. Turn out the dough onto the floured spot and knead very briefly. Pat the dough into a ½ inch thickness. Using a 3-inch cutter, cut out eight biscuits, gently patting any scraps together, if needed.

Place the biscuits in the prepared skillet with the sides touching (this will help them rise). Bake for 12 minutes, or until gloriously golden brown. Remove the biscuits from the oven and brush with the melted butter. Sprinkle the salt over the buttered biscuit tops.

**NOTES:** *Double this recipe and stash eight of the biscuits in the freezer. You will have these hospitable bites ready for unexpected company.*

# fiery mango jam

JAM IS ONE WAY WE UNIVERSALLY PRESERVE FRUITS WHEN THEY ARE IN ABUNDANCE. I am mad for mangoes. When mangoes are in season, I make batches and batches of this fruit spread. This jam is stupendous on toast or Rice Sopping Bread (page 145). I also like to spread it on a slice of Cardamom Cornbread (page 74) or Quick Tellicherry Buttermilk Biscuits (page 49). It can change your whole bagel-and-cream-cheese game in the morning, too.

**MAKES 1 QUART**

4 medium fresh mangoes, peeled, stoned, and cubed, or frozen mangoes, thawed (4 cups)

Zest of 2 lemons

6 tablespoons freshly squeezed lemon juice

1 tablespoon peeled, finely chopped fresh ginger

4 Thai chiles, finely chopped

2 1/2 cups fine granulated raw sugar (see notes)

Combine all of the ingredients in a heavy-bottomed pot. Cook over low heat, stirring often, taking care not to scorch, for 30 minutes. Using a spoon or spatula, drizzle a small bit of the jam on a cool plate. If the mixture is runny, continue to cook until thicker. If ready, the jam will appear glossy and thick. When the right consistency is reached, remove from the heat and pour the jam into a bowl to cool. Transfer to a storage container and cover. Store refrigerated for up to one month or process for canning.

**NOTES:** *Make a batch of this tropical jam omitting the pepper and use in Colonial Trifle (page 244). I like to use Zulka Morena Pure Cane Sugar for this and other recipes calling for granulated raw sugar.*

# tomato clove preserves

ALTHOUGH I SPEND MANY MORNINGS scouring the Atlanta area for specific ingredients, I am often blessed by my many farmer friends who drop by Spice to Table with their garden-fresh offerings. Being presented with vine-ripened, homegrown tomatoes during the peak of the hot Georgia summer is pure pleasure. The simplicity of the components in this recipe belies the wonderfully sophisticated flavors that result after the tomatoes and spices have cooked down. A dollop of this spiced tomato preserve becomes a ruby-colored jewel when served along with roasted lamb or venison. Tomato Clove Preserves also adds a bit of brilliance to a grilled cheese sandwich made with sharp cheddar on sourdough bread.

When my mother made these preserves, I would find reasons to meander through the kitchen just to catch a whiff of the heady clove and the sweet aroma of the tomatoes as they cooked down in a slow, low boil. I now find my son drawn to the same mysteriously alluring scent, ditching his backpack and propping himself up at the counter at Third Space to watch as I prepare this recipe. I am so happy to share my mother's recipe. Serving Tomato Clove Preserves never fails to flood my heart with sweet memories.

## TOMATO CLOVE PRESERVES

4 pounds of ripe tomatoes, peeled, seeded, and roughly chopped

1 cup white granulated sugar

1 teaspoon kosher salt

3/4 teaspoon clove powder

1/2 teaspoon freshly ground black peppercorns

1 teaspoon Kashmiri chili powder

Combine all of the ingredients in a large, heavy-bottomed pot. Bring to a boil over medium heat. Reduce heat to medium low and cook for 35 minutes, or until thickened. Store the jam in the refrigerator for up to two weeks.

# jeera water

GROWING UP IN KERALA THERE WAS ALWAYS *JEERA* WATER, made fresh every day at the crack of dawn, sitting at room temperature on the kitchen counter in an earthenware pot with a little spigot in it. We were encouraged to drink *jeera* water throughout the day. My mother, as well as many ayurvedic practitioners, advised that drinking ice-cold water caused constriction and was thus discouraged. Cumin seeds, called *jeera* in southern India, are thought to aid digestion and increase daily iron intake and balance the chakras. This water helped cool our bodies down in the sweltering, hot Indian summers and prevented dehydration. As a child I never enjoyed drinking *jeera* water; the taste was too medicinal. As an adult, I have acquired quite a taste for it. Continuing the tradition and to reap its health benefits, I frequently prepare *jeera* water for my home. My family drinks it throughout the day. It is a very simple recipe with huge therapeutic advantages.

**MAKES 6 SERVINGS**

6 cups water

6 teaspoons cumin seeds

In a 2-quart pot over medium heat, bring 6 cups of water to a boil with the cumin seeds in about 3 to 4 minutes. Lower the flame and simmer for 5 to 6 minutes until the water turns a pale yellow color. Strain the water and set aside in a water jar; serve at room temperature.

# ginger coffee

IN KERALA AND THROUGHOUT MUCH OF INDIA, WE HAVE MORE OF A TEA CULTURE than a coffee culture. In some parts of Kerala, dried ginger is placed in the bottom of the cup before adding the coffee, then the brew is sweetened with cane syrup or palm sugar. Gingered coffee has a unique taste and is a simple, yet interesting, way to experience how another culture indulges in coffee. Mornings are often hectic, and I usually set a timer to make sure the coffee does not steep too long and become bitter.

**MAKES 4 SERVINGS**

4 tablespoons ground coffee (your favorite kind)

2 teaspoons ginger powder

8 teaspoons cane syrup

Pour the ground coffee into a 6-cup French press. Bring 4 cups of water to a boil, then cool for 1 minute. Add the water to the French press and stir the brew. Steep for 3 to 4 minutes depending on the strength of coffee you prefer; 4 minutes will give you a robust brew. Slowly press the plunger, and pour the coffee into 4 cups. Add ½ teaspoon of dried ginger and 2 teaspoons of cane syrup to each cup and stir. Drink the coffee immediately.

**NOTE:** *Use this coffee to make the ice globes for Spicy Cold Old Monk (page 125).*

# hazel's fresh tomato juice cocktail

WHEN I WAS THIRTEEN, WE BRIEFLY LIVED IN GUJARAT in the northwestern region of India for a year before we moved to the United States. We lived in a town called Rajkot. Our home was within walking distance of St. Mary's School, a facility run by Jesuit priests where my brothers studied, and my school, Nirmala Convent, staffed by British and Portuguese nuns. My mother often cooked for the priests and nuns, and our home was always a welcoming place for them to visit. Once Mother Teresa visited our town during a drought in the region. Well, the priests decided that Mother Teresa must visit us on her way to a tree planting. After the phone call alerting my mom that the famous nun would be dropping by our house, I remember her being overjoyed with anticipation. The first thing my mother did was to whip up this refreshing tomato juice. It was a hot day, and she wanted to make sure Mother Teresa had a cold juice option if she didn't care for chai. The visit was brief, but she loved the juice. She asked my parents if she could take me along with her to the ceremony. I planted a neem tree with Mother Teresa that day. I have just one tattoo on my body and it is of a neem tree. My interaction with Mother Teresa all those years ago impacted my life in a most profound way.

**MAKES 4 SERVINGS**

½ pound Roma tomatoes, peeled and quartered

2 cups cold water

½ cup white granulated sugar

Place the tomatoes, cold water, and sugar in a blender and pulse until smooth. Strain and chill the cocktail. Serve in a chilled glass.

# atlanta buttermilk peach lassi

LASSI IS A MUCH-LOVED DRINK ACROSS INDIA, particularly the Punjab region, and is served any time of day. A central component in a lassi is yogurt. My abiding love for buttermilk got me to concoct an Atlanta-style lassi with sweet peaches. Plums work wonderfully well, too, in this yogurt and buttermilk drink.

**MAKES 2 DRINKS**

1½ cups peeled and chopped ripe peaches or frozen peaches

½ cup crushed ice

½ cup plain whole yogurt, chilled

½ cup buttermilk

1 tablespoon honey

Pinch of kosher salt

Pinch of cardamom powder

Purée the peaches in a blender until almost smooth. Add the ice, yogurt, buttermilk, honey, salt, and cardamom and frappe or blend to combine. Serve at once.

# papaya lime cocktail

ON MY RARE MORNINGS OFF, I ENJOY LOUNGING AROUND AND CATCHING UP ON MY READING while sipping this brightly flavored, sweetened juice drink. Papaya contains enzymes that promote the digestion of proteins, making it an excellent addition for morning nutrition.

**MAKES FOUR 8-OUNCE SERVINGS**

2 cups fresh peeled papaya, seeded and diced

4 tablespoons agave syrup

Juice of 2 limes

Crushed ice, for serving

Lime wedges, for garnish, if desired

Combine the papaya, agave, 2 cups of water, and lime juice in a blender and pulse to purée. Serve over crushed ice. Garnish with fresh lime wedges.

# lychee strawberry smoothie

*GO! GO! GO! SOME MORNINGS WE SIMPLY HAVE TO HIT THE GROUND RUNNING.* Having canned lychees in the pantry and berries and yogurt in the refrigerator is a lifesaver when you have just got to go *now*. Toss everything in the blender, give it a quick whir, pour it out, and head on out the door and face the day. An additional bonus of this healthful smoothie is that it stays nice and cool in a thermos for a tasty lunch-box treat. Shake it really well, then enjoy.

Sweet lychees are plump pink-skinned Asian fruits with translucent opalescent white flesh and a seed in the center. In canned fruit cocktails, lychees can add that special flavor that some kids adore.

On slower-paced mornings, this smoothie pairs well with Spice to Table Date Oatmeal (page 33), for a breakfast that will surely stave off late-morning munchies.

**MAKES FOUR 12-OUNCE SMOOTHIES**

2½ cups (one 20-ounce can) peeled and seeded lychees in syrup

2 cups fresh or frozen strawberries (½ pound), washed and hulled

1 cup (8 ounces) plain Greek-style yogurt

2 cups ice

Combine the lychees (with the syrup), strawberries, and yogurt in a blender. Blend until well mixed, about 2 to 3 minutes. Add ice; pulse until the mixture attains a smooth consistency.

**NOTES:** *When strawberries are at their peak season, whip up a batch of these smoothies, portion the mixture into individual servings, and pop them into the freezer. On a busy morning, empty one of the frozen drinks into a blender, give it a quick pulse, and you are on your way, quick as a wink!*

# plate lunches &
# simple pleasures

*Atlanta is a lunch town. From big three-course meals and large sandwiches to quick, light, and refreshing pauses, the midday repast is a vital part of this city's culinary culture. The South in general values the long lunch: my American travels enamored me of New Orleanians' way of turning lingering lunches into all-day affairs.*

Fun-loving friends gather over impromptu lunches to celebrate life's milestones. I love the randomness of some lunches: the great happenstance of bumping into a friend and tossing together a quick salad or sandwich, catching up with each other's lives, and taking a brief walk down memory lane.

Atlanta's famed dining destination roadway, Buford Highway, is lined with buffets of international origins as well as more traditional blue-collar, Deep South fare. Lunch boxes and Sunday dinner tables are filled and set with equal care. Celebratory luncheons are held for graduates or the betrothed; they are de rigueur

for Georgia—a state that, after all, has a town named Social Circle. We like to eat together at midday whether it's to grab a salad and chat or undertake a long, lingering lunch that refuels the body and spirit. Down here, lunch is one of life's simple pleasures not to be skipped.

At Spice to Table we have implemented what is commonly referred to as the "Meat and Three" lunch. Customers can choose one meat item, such as our famous Kerala Fried Chicken, spicy Mint Masala Roasted Chicken, or Railways Beef Curry, and then fill the three side-dish slots on the cafeteria-style tray with the likes of Red Cabbage Thoren, Mess O' Greens, and Green Bean Verakka

# gingered beef *and* potato croquettes *with* savoy *and* green apple slaw

A FAVORITE INDIAN STREET FOOD, potato croquettes are commonly known as *aloo tikki*. They basically consist of potatoes, mixed with spices and a binder, formed into a patty, then deep-fried and served hot. Like many recipes from my homeland, there are many variations. In the American South, I discovered similar dishes like potato pancakes and salmon croquettes. Jumping on another opportunity to create a South by South–inspired recipe, I developed these beef croquettes to be served as a quick meal to satisfy all ages. There is a vegetarian version for Golden Potato Croquettes on page 139.

2 cups plus 1 tablespoon canola oil

2 medium shallots, finely chopped

2 tablespoons peeled, finely chopped ginger

2 teaspoons freshly ground black peppercorns

2 teaspoons granulated garlic powder

1½ teaspoons kosher salt

1½ pounds lean ground sirloin

2 medium gold potatoes (½ pound), peeled, boiled, and smashed into small pieces

4 eggs, yolks and whites separated

2 cups panko breadcrumbs

**MAKES 12 TO 15 CROQUETTES**

In a medium skillet, heat 1 tablespoon of the canola oil over medium heat. Add the shallots and cook, stirring until the shallots are translucent, about 3 to 5 minutes. Add the ginger, black pepper, garlic powder, and salt, cooking while stirring for about a minute.

Add the ground sirloin and cook over medium heat, stirring occasionally, until the sirloin is fully cooked (no longer pink) and the liquid is evaporated, about 8 minutes. Set beef aside in a large bowl to cool for about 15 minutes.

Once cooled, add the smashed potatoes and egg yolks to the sirloin and mix together by hand so that all the ingredients are well combined. Mold the sirloin mixture into 12 to 15 teardrop-shaped patties and set aside.

In a small bowl, beat the egg whites and set aside.

Put the breadcrumbs in a medium bowl.

Take each meat patty and dip in the egg whites, getting a nice wet coat on them, then coat the meat patties with the breadcrumbs and set aside until ready to fry.

In a large, deep frying pan on medium heat, heat 3 inches of oil to 300°F. Fry the croquettes until golden brown for about 4 to 5 minutes, turning to brown on all sides.

Remove from oil with a slotted spoon and place on a plate lined with paper towels to absorb the excess oil.

## SAVOY AND GREEN APPLE SLAW

SAVOY CABBAGE HAS CRINKLY, green ombré leaves that take on a beautiful ribbon appearance and texture when thinly sliced. Simply dressed in a sweet garlic dressing, the cabbage ribbons wrap themselves around tart green apple matchsticks for a lovely salad.

**MAKES 6 SERVINGS**

½ head savoy cabbage, thinly sliced (see notes)

2 Granny Smith apples, julienned

½ cup mayonnaise

1 teaspoon very finely chopped garlic

1 tablespoon white granulated sugar

½ teaspoon kosher salt

In a large bowl, mix the cabbage, apples, mayonnaise, garlic, sugar, and salt and set aside to cool in the refrigerator for about 30 minutes. Toss and serve.

**NOTES:** *This sensationally easy salad is the one to turn to when that potluck dinner slipped your mind. At the market look for savoy cabbage with dark leaves. As the cabbage ages, often the outer leaves are removed revealing the paler inner leaves; this can be a sign that it has been quite a while since it was picked. Try napa cabbage in this slaw if savoy cabbage is unavailable.*

# kerala fried chicken *and* low country rice waffles *with* spicy syrup

ALTHOUGH THE AMERICAN SOUTH HAS LAID CLAIM TO FRIED CHICKEN—and rightfully so—nearly every culture has a similar bird dish. There is a true universality to brining a bird to plump it, dredging it through seasoned flour, followed by deep frying. I grew up eating fried chicken in my mother's kitchen in a South on the other side of the world. When I moved to the American South, I happily discovered many fried-chicken-loving kindred spirits. Guests often assume that my fried chicken comes from my exposure to the cuisine of the American South. It's always fun explaining to them that it is actually part of my Keralan heritage.

I wanted to create a satisfying dish that would showcase both my Souths, and I thought the idea of Carolina low country rice waffles paired with my version of Kerala-style fried chicken would fit the bill perfectly by flipping the script on a soul food classic. What better way to marry—and consummate—these dishes than by binding them with spiced syrup? For breakfast and brunch, I favor the universal favorite, maple syrup, and for lunch and dinner, I lean toward cane syrup for its deeper flavor. Turns out that this singular dish, which brought together my two Souths, put me on the map locally, nationally, and internationally.

I like to make the syrup when I set the chicken to marinating. That way everything has a bit of time to infuse with the bold flavors of Kerala before I start showing my Atlanta chops. For the lightest waffles, I let the batter sit for an hour before cooking it in a waffle iron. I also like to make sure I have given the waffle iron ample time to heat thoroughly for the crispest, most golden crust. Novice fryers will benefit from keeping a thermometer on hand to check the temperature of the oil and to make sure the chicken is cooked all the way to the bone.

# KERALA FRIED CHICKEN

2 cups buttermilk

10 garlic cloves

6 whole serrano peppers, seeded if desired

1 bunch fresh cilantro (about 1 cup)

1 bunch fresh mint (about 1/2 cup)

2 tablespoons plus 1 teaspoon kosher salt

8 boneless, skinless chicken thighs (about 3 pounds)

Canola oil, for frying

4 cups unbleached all-purpose flour

2 tablespoons coconut oil, melted

2 stems fresh curry leaves, for garnish

In a blender, combine the buttermilk, garlic, peppers, cilantro, mint, and 2 tablespoons of the salt and purée until smooth. Place the chicken in a large container with lid, and pour the buttermilk marinade over the chicken. Toss the chicken in the marinade, making sure it is well coated. Cover and refrigerate for at least 18 hours and up to 24 hours.

When ready to fry the chicken, fill a large cast-iron skillet with 1 inch of oil and heat gently over medium heat until the oil reaches 350°F. Place a cooling rack over a rimmed baking sheet and set aside. Combine the flour and 1 teaspoon of salt in a shallow dish and set aside.

While the oil is heating, remove the chicken from the marinade and gently shake off the excess marinade. Dredge each piece of chicken in the flour, coating thoroughly.

Place the chicken in the hot oil, taking care not to crowd the pieces. Cook the chicken until it is deep golden brown and cooked through, about 4 minutes on each side, or until a meat thermometer reads 165°F. Drain the chicken on the cooling rack and drizzle with the melted coconut oil.

Dip the curry leaves in the hot frying oil until crisp, about 10 to 15 seconds. Set on the cooling rack.

## LOW COUNTRY RICE WAFFLES

1½ cups unbleached all-purpose flour

½ cup white rice flour

2 tablespoons packed light-brown sugar

2 teaspoons baking powder

2 teaspoons baking soda

6 to 8 green cardamom pods, crushed

1 teaspoon kosher salt

2 large eggs

2½ cups buttermilk

6 tablespoons (3/4 stick) unsalted butter, melted

½ cup cooked white jasmine rice

Nonstick pan spray

In a large bowl, whisk together the flour, rice flour, brown sugar, baking powder, baking soda, cardamom, and salt. In a separate bowl, whisk the eggs. Add the buttermilk and melted butter to the eggs and whisk well to combine.

Slowly whisk the wet mixture into the dry ingredients. Add the cooked rice and whisk just until combined. Cover the batter and let it rest for 1 hour at room temperature.

When ready to cook the waffles, heat the waffle iron and spray generously with oil. Ladle about ½ cup of batter into the waffle iron, and cook until crisp and golden, about 4 to 5 minutes.

To assemble the dish, place the waffle on a plate, place the fried chicken on top of the waffle, and top with fried curry leaves; serve the syrup on the side.

**NOTES:** *Use leftover rice for these crisp waffles, or cook 1/4 cup rice in 1/2 cup water to get the amount of cooked rice needed in the waffle recipe.*

## SPICY SYRUP

2 tablespoons whole cumin seeds, coarsely ground

2 tablespoons whole coriander seeds, coarsely ground

1 teaspoon crushed red pepper flakes

2 cups maple syrup or cane syrup

In a small skillet over medium-high heat, toast the cumin, coriander, and red pepper flakes until fragrant, about 1 minute. Whisk the toasted spices into the syrup. Let the spices infuse the syrup for up to 24 hours at room temperature.

# country captain *with* lemon relish

COUNTRY CAPTAIN IS A DISH WITH A RICH CULINARY NARRATIVE. After many conversations with guests and home cooks at Cardamom Hill, my first restaurant in Atlanta, I became fascinated with the diners' memories of their heritage recipes for Country Captain. Many of the native southern cooks shared family versions that have been handed down for generations. I was also intrigued by the original recipe's connection to India. Every time I make this dish, I replay in my mind a tale stretching from its fabled origins in India through its journey to the American South with a certain seafaring "country captain" to its various interpretations in countless kitchens across the decades. I like to imagine a British seaman coming to America more than a century ago: he reminisces about a memorable chicken curry he had enjoyed on his tour of India and decides to re-create it, using locally available ingredients. With this recipe, I'm bringing Country Captain back to its roots, completing a circle that ties my Indian heritage to a beloved Charleston, South Carolina, dish. I like to serve this wildly popular dish over Carolina Gold rice (page 93) with Lemon Relish and a hearty side of Mess O' Greens (page 85).

# COUNTRY CAPTAIN

1 chicken (3 to 4 pounds), cut into 10 pieces (see notes)

3 teaspoons kosher salt, divided

1 teaspoon freshly ground black peppercorns

1/4 cup canola oil

1 large yellow onion, roughly chopped

4 celery stalks, roughly chopped

1 medium red bell pepper, seeded and chopped

1 medium green bell pepper, seeded and chopped

6 garlic cloves, finely chopped

1 tablespoon peeled, finely chopped fresh ginger

1/3 cup blanched sliced almonds, divided

2 tablespoons garam masala

1 tablespoon coriander powder

1 tablespoon sweet paprika powder

1 teaspoon turmeric powder

2 cups (16 ounces) peeled, chopped tomatoes (fresh, if in season, or canned)

1 tablespoon tomato paste

2 tablespoons cane syrup

1/3 cup dried Zante currants or raisins, divided

1/3 cup frozen, grated fresh coconut, thawed

Season the chicken all over with 1 teaspoon of the salt and 1 teaspoon of the pepper.

In a large (5-quart) Dutch oven, heat the oil over medium heat until it reaches 250°F. Add the chicken to the hot oil, skin-side down, and cook, turning once or twice, until golden brown, about 10 minutes. Transfer the chicken to a plate and set aside. Reduce the heat to medium low.

To the pan drippings, add the onions, celery, the red and green bell peppers, garlic, ginger, and one-half of the almonds. Cook, stirring occasionally, until the onions are translucent, about 8 to 10 minutes. Add the garam masala, coriander, paprika, turmeric, and remaining salt, and cook, stirring frequently, until the spices are aromatic, about 3 to 4 minutes.

Add the tomatoes, tomato paste, cane syrup, and one-half of the currants. Stir well, reduce heat to low, cover and simmer, stirring occasionally, until the mixture cooks down to a chunky sauce, about 25 minutes.

Meanwhile, heat the oven to 350°F. Add the reserved chicken and any accumulated juices to the Dutch oven, nestling the chicken into the sauce. Cover and bake for about an hour, or until the chicken is tender. Garnish with remaining currants and almonds and the grated fresh coconut. Serve warm with the Lemon Relish.

**NOTES:** *I like to purchase whole chickens and break them down myself. I end up with the back and scraps to use in stock, and it is much less expensive per pound than packaged cut-up chicken. I begin by cutting out the backbone with poultry shears. I disjoint the thighs next and remove the leg quarters and separate the drumsticks from the thighs. Then, with a good bit of force, I flatten the breast and cut it into two halves. Off come the wings. Then I cut the breasts in halves, crosswise, producing four breast pieces. These smaller breast pieces cook more evenly and allow more diners to have a piece of white meat.*

## LEMON RELISH

MAKES 10 SERVINGS

2 tablespoons canola oil

1 teaspoon black or brown mustard seeds

2 teaspoons turmeric powder

2 teaspoons Kitchari chili powder

1/2 teaspoon asafoetida powder

2 teaspoons kosher salt

2 tablespoons white granulated sugar

1 tablespoon peeled, finely chopped fresh ginger

5 Meyer lemons, cut in half lengthwise and seeded; cut each half lengthwise into 4 slices, and cut each slice into 3 pieces

In a medium heavy-bottomed pan over medium-high heat, add the oil, then add the mustard seeds and wait until the seeds pop, about 30 seconds. Add all the turmeric powder, Kitchari chili powder, asafoetida powder, salt, sugar, and ginger. Cook the spices, sugar, and ginger, stirring constantly for a minute. Reduce the flame to a medium heat; add the lemons and mix well so all the spices coat the lemons. Add the water and mix well; cook, stirring occasionally, until all of the liquid evaporates, about 8 minutes. Remove from heat and serve at room temperature.

# southern-style pork vindaloo *and* **green bean verakka** *with* cardamom cornbread

VINDALOO IS A RECIPE THAT BEST REPRESENTS KERALA'S DIVERSE CULINARY influences, and it also reflects many of my own. My first encounter with the tongue-searing pork *vindaloo* served in many Indian restaurants in the US was a bit jarring. I remember thinking how vastly different it was from the pork *vindaloo* I grew up eating in Kerala. Like many dishes traveling across the seas amid many interpretations, I feel *vindaloo* got lost in translation.

Vindaloo was originally inspired by a Portuguese dish, *carne de vinha d'alhos* (meat with wine and garlic), with the wine substituted with palm wine vinegar. This dish was introduced to Kerala and Goa by Portuguese sailors who stored chunks of meat in wine barrels on the ship; the wine would turn to vinegar and thus preserve the meat for long journeys. When they got to shore, the sailors would add local spices to the meat and cook a stew. This dish has many nuances: your palate experiences the tang from the vinegar, sweetness from the sugar, heat generated more from garlic than chiles, and a touch of bitterness from ground mustard seeds. Here, sugar, hot paprika, and a generous amount of garlic transport the pork roast to a faraway land. Choose a nice fatty pork shoulder, or Boston butt, to ensure lusciousness.

I particularly enjoy the flavor of the rich sauce once it seeps down into Cardamom Cornbread. Serving it this way brings to the plate a little something extra; my Louisiana friends refer to this as *lagniappe*.

## SOUTHERN-STYLE PORK VINDALOO

MAKES 6 SERVINGS

12 garlic cloves

1 tablespoon hot paprika

1 teaspoon brown mustard seeds

2 teaspoons white granulated sugar

1 teaspoon kosher salt

1 tablespoon tomato paste

1/2 cup white vinegar

1/4 cup canola oil

1 medium red onion, chopped

1/2 teaspoon crushed red pepper flakes

2 pounds pork shoulder (Boston butt), cut into 1/2-pound pieces

In a food processor or blender, combine the garlic, paprika, mustard seeds, sugar, salt, tomato paste, vinegar, and 1/4 cup water. Blend the mixture until smooth.

In a large skillet, heat the oil over medium-high heat. Add the onion and red pepper flakes and cook, stirring, until the onion is golden brown, about 5 to 6 minutes. Add the pork and the blended sauce. Stir well to coat the pork, cover, reduce heat to low, and cook until the pork is falling apart and the sauce is thick and lush, about 45 minutes. During this time, start making the cornbread. After 45 minutes, if needed, uncover the pork, raise the heat, and bring the sauce to a boil to thicken it, about 3 to 5 minutes.

**NOTES:** *For those who abstain from pork, boneless untrimmed leg of lamb can be substituted with great results.*

## GREEN BEAN VERAKKA

*Verakka* is simply an Indian stir-fry. Here, green beans cut into beads are paired with savory thyme and quickly cooked in oil in which cumin and mustard seeds have been popped.

2 tablespoons coconut oil

1 teaspoon brown mustard seeds

1 teaspoon cumin seeds

1 pound (about 4 cups) green beans, trimmed and cut into 1/8-inch rounds

2 teaspoons fresh thyme leaves

1 teaspoon kosher salt

MAKES 4 SERVINGS

Heat the coconut oil in a medium wok over medium-high heat. Add the mustard and cumin seeds; when the seeds begin to pop, add the green beans, thyme, and salt. Add 1/4 cup water and cook, stirring, until the beans are just tender and the water has evaporated, about 4 minutes.

## CARDAMOM CORNBREAD

I learned to bake cornbread here in Atlanta. My addition of cardamom and a good bit of black pepper just takes it a little farther South—to India.

5 tablespoons melted unsalted butter, divided

2 cups cornmeal

2 teaspoons green cardamom powder

1 teaspoon kosher salt

1 1/2 teaspoons white granulated sugar

1/2 teaspoon baking soda

2 large eggs

2 cups buttermilk

**MAKES ONE 9-INCH PAN, 8 TO 10 SERVINGS**

Heat the oven to 425°F. Grease a 9-inch cast-iron skillet with 1 tablespoon of the butter. In a large bowl, mix together the cornmeal, cardamom, salt, sugar, and baking soda. In a separate bowl, whisk the eggs and buttermilk together. Pour the buttermilk and eggs into the large bowl with the dry ingredients and mix well. Add the remaining melted butter and whisk. Pour the batter into the skillet and bake for 15 to 20 minutes. Serve warm.

# black cardamom smothered pork chop

I LOVE SOUL FOOD AND RELISH THE COMFORTING FEELINGS evoked by eating my favorite southern soul-food dishes. I'm fascinated by how this cuisine connects several cultures—Africa and the Americas as well as the West Indies.

There are certain dishes that are so special that I hesitate to alter them too much, as rooted as they are in time, place, and history. Let's face it: it's difficult to improve a classic smothered pork chop. So in every way possible, I try to preserve the integrity of such recipes by staying true to the tradition while also adding a subtle new experience of flavor. In this recipe, I chose to highlight black cardamom, an underused spice in most pantries, which imparts a smoky, pungent flavor. I first season the chops with the spice blend and then add the remainder to the gravy. After much trial and error, the black cardamom version of a southern soul-food pork chop was born.

I serve these bone-in pork chops wallowing in black cardamom and clove-spiked gravy with fluffy white rice and Mess O' Greens (page 85). It might be a good idea to make a batch of Tellicherry Buttermilk Biscuits (page 49) or Rice Sopping Bread (page 145) because there is serious sopping to be done when finishing up a plate of this gravy.

4 bone-in pork chops, 1 inch thick

2 tablespoons Spice Blend, divided

4 tablespoons canola oil

2 tablespoons unsalted butter

2 large yellow onions, halved and thinly sliced

6 garlic cloves, finely chopped

1½ tablespoons unbleached all-purpose flour

2 cups chicken stock

¼ cup buttermilk

Sprinkle pork chops on both sides using one-half of the spice blend. Save the remaining spice blend for the smothering sauce.

Heat the vegetable oil in a large skillet over medium heat; brown the pork chops well on both sides, about 5 minutes per side. Transfer to a plate.

Discard the grease from the pan and melt the butter in the same skillet. Reduce the heat to medium low and add the onions. Cook the onions until very brown and caramelized, stirring occasionally, about 15 minutes.

Stir in the garlic and the remaining spice blend and cook over medium heat for 1 minute. Stir in the flour and cook, stirring constantly for 2 minutes. Pour the chicken stock into the skillet and stir, scraping up all of the browned bits and taking care to break up any lumps of flour. Stir in any juices that have accumulated on the plate holding the pork chops and then add the buttermilk. Bring sauce to a simmer, then reduce the heat to low. Cook, stirring occasionally, until the onions begin to break down and the sauce becomes a thick gravy, 15 to 20 minutes.

Nestle the pork chops into the sauce, spooning sauce over the chops to coat. Simmer the chops, covered, until tender and cooked through at the bone, about 20 minutes.

## SPICE BLEND

1 black cardamom pod

1 tablespoon whole black peppercorns

8 whole dried cloves

2 teaspoons kosher salt

Coarsely grind the cardamom pod, black peppercorns, cloves, and salt together with a mortar and pestle or spice grinder.

# fresh thyme fish cakes

THYME IS NOT AN HERB I WAS ACCUSTOMED TO before I moved to the States. Since moving to Atlanta, I have fallen head over heels for the different varieties of thyme available at nurseries—their various flavors and variegated colors. Little pots of fresh thyme marching down the center of a table at a luncheon make a fragrant and beautiful centerpiece and are wonderful party favors for guests to take home for their kitchen windowsills.

These herbaceous fish cakes are perfect for luncheons. They are light and fresh and easy on the hostess for their prepare-ahead quality. When paired with a tossed salad dressed with Cardamom Honey Lime Dressing (page 98), they make a good-looking plate. Honeydew Bavarian (page 227) will round out the menu for a lovely luncheon.

**MAKES 8 CAKES**

2 pounds cod steaks

2 tablespoons coconut oil

1 medium red onion, finely chopped

3 serrano chiles, seeded and finely chopped

2 tablespoons fresh thyme leaves

1 tablespoon peeled, finely chopped fresh ginger

4 garlic cloves, finely chopped

1 teaspoon kosher salt

2 cups panko breadcrumbs, divided

4 eggs, yolks and whites separated (only two yolks are used)

2 tablespoons mayonnaise

½ cup canola oil

In a medium pot, bring 1 cup of water to a simmer. Add the cod and cook covered over low heat, for 10 minutes. Transfer the fish to a medium bowl and discard the water.

Flake the fish into pieces about the size of jumbo lump crabmeat.

Return the pot to medium heat and add the coconut oil. Add the onions and cook, stirring, until translucent, about 3 to 4 minutes. Add the serrano chiles, thyme, ginger, garlic, and salt. Cook and stir for 2 minutes. Add this onion mixture to the cod. Add ½ cup of the breadcrumbs, 2 egg yolks, and the mayonnaise. Very gently, fold the ingredients together. Form 8 cakes.

Line a sheet pan with parchment paper. In a shallow bowl, beat the egg whites until frothy. Place the remaining breadcrumbs in a shallow dish. Dip each cake in the egg white and then thoroughly coat in the breadcrumbs. Set the coated cakes on the lined pan; cover and refrigerate for ½ hour, or up to a day, prior to cooking.

When ready to cook, heat the oven to 350°F.

Heat the oil in a medium skillet. Fry the cakes on each side for 1 minute in batches so as not to crowd the pan, then return the cakes to the sheet pan.

Bake the cakes until golden brown and crispy, about 20 minutes. Serve piping hot.

# whole roasted fish *with* gullah country moppin' sauce

ONE AFTERNOON MY FRIEND Sid Feagin delivered to me a sample of his amazing product, Gullah Gravy Low Country Moppin' Sauce, and asked me to play around with it. Created by his grandfather, Carlton Feagin, in South Carolina around 1960—long before Sid was born—the goal was to create the perfect mop sauce. To the uninitiated, mop sauce is a thin liquid used to baste a food cooking over low heat for long periods of time. Ingredients often include some combination of tomato juice, vinegar, apple cider, and/or beer. During cooking, food is literally "mopped" with this sauce to prevent it from drying out and to enhance flavor. The mop sauce is sometimes served at the table as well. People often commented that if Sid's grandfather's calloused hands weren't working at the steel mill, they were stirring his sauce. Folks traveled from miles around to buy his sauce. It was sold in glass jugs, empty liquor bottles, or mason jars and brought home to be slathered on everything—pork, chicken, seafood, venison, and beef. I decided to try it in a fish recipe. I dedicate this dish to Sid and his grandfather Carlton.

3 trout (1½ pounds), dressed

½ cup extra virgin olive oil

1 teaspoon kosher salt

1 teaspoon turmeric powder

1 teaspoon cayenne pepper powder (if you want to avoid the heat, use a teaspoon of sweet paprika)

1 teaspoon garlic powder

2 lemons, each sliced into 4 rings

8 sprigs fresh thyme

1 pint cherry tomatoes

1 cup Gullah Country Moppin' Sauce

**MAKES 6 SERVINGS**

Heat the oven to 400°F. Pat the fresh fish dry inside and out with paper towels. Make 3 diagonal cuts through the skin on each side of the fish. Place the fish on a rimmed sheet pan. Generously and evenly pour the olive oil over the fish.

Season the fish inside and out with the salt, turmeric, cayenne powder, and garlic powder. Gently insert the lemon rings and thyme sprigs into the fish's belly. Scatter the tomatoes in the pan.

Pour 1 cup of Gullah Country Moppin' Sauce over the fish.

Roast the fish for 25 to 30 minutes or until a thermometer inserted into the thickest part reads 140°F. Baste the fish every 8 to 10 minutes.

Remove from the oven and serve immediately.

# GULLAH COUNTRY MOPPIN' SAUCE

MOP THIS CAROLINA-INSPIRED sauce on anything that will hold still, from a slice of white bread to roasted eggplant.

2½ cups apple cider vinegar

1 tablespoon prepared yellow mustard

1 (8-ounce) can tomato juice

1 cup ketchup

1 tablespoon Worcestershire sauce

5 paper-thin, ¼-inch-wide slices of lemon rind (only the colored rind, not the white pith)

2 tablespoons fresh lemon juice

2 teaspoons crushed red pepper

2 teaspoons fresh coarsely ground black peppercorns

3 tablespoons unsalted butter

Dash of hot pepper sauce

**MAKES ABOUT 1 QUART**

Whisk ingredients together in a sauce pot on medium flame and simmer for 15 minutes, stirring constantly. Remove from heat and cool. Store this mopping sauce refrigerated in a jar for up to six months.

# mess o' greens *with* ham hocks *and* jalapeños

ONE OF MY FAVORITE CHEFS and dearest friends is Steven Satterfield of Atlanta's Miller Union restaurant. No one makes a bowl of greens, pot licker, and cornbread like Steven does. This dish is dedicated to Steven for all he has taught me about southern cuisine and for introducing me to the work of the "godmother of southern food," Edna Lewis. Her book, *The Taste of Country Cooking*, is ever at hand in my kitchen and has served as a guide as I learned to navigate kitchens in Georgia. The tutelage of these two helped me develop my way of cooking greens with a bit of cane syrup, vinegar, and jalapeños.

2 tablespoons unsalted butter

2 tablespoons olive oil

1 large onion, chopped

2 garlic cloves, finely chopped

2 jalapeños, seeded and finely chopped

1 pound smoked ham hocks

1/2 pound turnip greens, washed and drained

1/2 pound mustard greens, washed and drained

1 pound collard greens, washed and drained

1 1/2 teaspoons kosher salt

1 teaspoon freshly grated nutmeg

3 tablespoons cane syrup

1/2 cup rice wine vinegar

**MAKES 6 SERVINGS**

Heat a large Dutch oven over medium heat and melt the butter with the olive oil.

Add the onion, garlic, and jalapeño. Cook, stirring occasionally, until the onions are translucent, about 4 to 5 minutes. Add the smoked ham hocks, greens, salt, nutmeg, cane syrup, and vinegar; stir well.

Add 3 cups of water and bring to a boil. Reduce heat and cover. Simmer for about 2 hours until tender (maybe sooner depending on the natural tenderness of the greens).

# goat confit sliders *with* serrano mango sauce

WHO DOESN'T LOVE A GREAT SLIDER with a cold beer while watching a ball-game? I grew up in a South where goat was a celebrated meat, much like the pig is in the American South. Like soccer or even cricket, goat has only recently found its way into the mainstream in the United States. Here in the Deep South, we are slowly but surely discovering that goat meat recipes deserve to be celebrated and explored. Goat is a low-fat, high-protein meat that is not at all gamey. In fact, many people mistake it for beef. The flavor is comparable to well-prepared venison. I predict that soon enough tailgating with goat will be setting fire to SWAC and SEC athletic competitions.

In this recipe, the goat meat is cooked down with star anise, allspice, and bay leaves and then removed from the bone, shredded, and dressed with a garlic, serrano chile, and mango sauce. Bring these bad-boy sliders to the next big game, and you'll become a tailgating legend!

2 cups olive oil

4 cups (32 ounces) vegetable stock

4 bay leaves

8 garlic cloves, finely chopped

8 whole star anise

12 whole allspice

1 tablespoon whole black peppercorns

1 tablespoon kosher salt

1 goat leg (3 to 4 pounds) (see notes)

1 cup Serrano Mango Sauce

24 small Hawaiian-style buns

Heat the oven to 225°F. In a large roasting pan, combine the oil, vegetable stock, bay leaves, garlic, star anise, allspice, peppercorns, and salt. Add the goat leg; the liquid should just cover the meat. Cover the pan tightly with foil and place it in the oven to roast for 1½ hours. Turn the meat over, and roast, covered, until the meat is very tender and falling off the bone, about an additional 1½ hours.

Remove the meat from the pan. Over medium heat, reduce the accumulated juices by one-half. In a separate bowl, shred the meat then add the reduction to the meat. Assemble the sliders. Spread each bun with a bit of Serrano Mango Sauce and fill with the shredded meat.

**NOTES:** *Get your butcher to cut the leg into a shank and a larger upper piece so it will fit into your roasting pan.*

## SERRANO MANGO SAUCE

I FORESEE THIS SAUCE FINDING ITS WAY ONTO ALL SORTS OF SANDWICHES and spooned over rotisserie chicken some hurried afternoon.

1 cup fresh or frozen mango, cubed

1 serrano chile, slit in half lengthwise

1 garlic clove

1 tablespoon white granulated sugar

½ teaspoon kosher salt

Place all of the ingredients in a blender or food processor with ¼ cup water and blend for 1 minute, or until the mixture is the consistency of ketchup. Serve immediately or refrigerate for up to 2 days.

# masala lamb burgers *with* mint chutney

GROWING UP IN INDIA, I enjoyed eating lots of lamb and came to adore grilled, minced lamb in particular. These days, like most Americans, I know few things that are better than a great burger cooked over a flame. So, what better way to pay homage to the best of both countries' grillers than with a lamb burger? Since lamb can be a bit strong tasting, diners new to eating lamb will find the masala blend of fresh mint and cilantro in this recipe mitigates some of lamb's inherent gaminess. Dressed with Mint Chutney, these burgers offer a delicious alternative to Americans' much-loved grilled beef burgers.

1½ pounds ground lamb

1 medium red onion, finely chopped

½ cup fresh mint, finely chopped

2 serrano chiles, seeded and finely chopped

1 teaspoon very finely chopped garlic

1 teaspoon cumin seeds, coarsely ground

2 teaspoons coriander powder

½ teaspoon ginger powder

2 tablespoons chickpea flour (see notes)

1 teaspoon kosher salt

Vegetable oil for grill rack or pan

6 brioche buns, toasted

6 leaves Bibb lettuce

1 large tomato, cut into 6 slices

1 large red onion, cut into 6 slices

**MAKES 6 BURGERS**

In a large bowl, mix the lamb, onion, mint, chiles, garlic, cumin, coriander, ginger, chickpea flour, and the salt with your hands until everything is combined.

Heat a grill or grill pan. Brush the grill rack or pan with vegetable oil.

Form 6 patties, about ¼ pound each. Grill over medium heat for about 4 to 5 minutes on each side, or until desired doneness. An internal temperature of 160°F is considered medium rare. Serve on toasted brioche with lettuce, tomato, red onion, and mint chutney.

**NOTES:** *Chickpea flour, also known as garbanzo bean flour or besan, is made from either raw or roasted ground chickpeas. The raw variety is slightly bitter, while the roasted is more flavorful. It is gluten free and higher in protein than many other flours.*

## MINT CHUTNEY

KEEP THIS CHUTNEY HANDY; it can brighten up a world of dishes. Think of it as a cousin to Italy's *gremolata* or Argentina's *chimichurri*.

1 small shallot, peeled and roughly chopped

1 cup mint leaves

1 cup cilantro leaves

2 Thai chiles, slit in half lengthwise

1 tablespoon fresh lime juice

Zest of one lime

1 teaspoon kosher salt

½ cup grated fresh coconut

½ cup water

**MAKES 1 CUP**

In a blender, combine all the ingredients and grind for 3 to 4 minutes on a low speed. The chutney should be a coarse consistency.

# chervil lime lobster salad roll

I KNOW, LOBSTER ROLLS ARE CONSIDERED A NEW ENGLAND DELICACY, not the least bit southern. And some might say adding garlic, chervil, lime juice, and crushed red pepper flakes is craziness, a travesty. Well, I contend that this recipe is more Miami than Boston, and I say give it a try! It will be well worth expanding your boundaries.

MAKES 4 ROLLS

1/2 cup mayonnaise

1 teaspoon very finely chopped garlic

1/2 cup chopped fresh chervil (see notes)

3 tablespoons fresh lime juice

1/2 teaspoon kosher salt

1/2 teaspoon crushed red pepper flakes

1 1/2 pounds (about 3 cups) cooked lobster meat, roughly chopped (see notes)

2 celery stalks, finely chopped

4 hot dog rolls (or similar buns), top split, lightly toasted

1 tablespoon unsalted butter, melted

In a large bowl, combine the mayonnaise, garlic, chervil, lime juice, salt, and pepper flakes. Fold the lobster and celery into the chervil-lime mayonnaise. Refrigerate mixture for 15 to 20 minutes for the flavors to mingle.

Brush inside of each roll with melted butter and fill with the lobster salad.

**NOTES:** *In Florida and along the warmer southern Atlantic coast, a variety of lobster called spiny or rock lobster is readily available. Unlike Maine lobster, which offers meat from the claws, body, and tail, their southern cousins provide only tail meat. The taste of any lobster may vary depending on where and when it is harvested. In this recipe, the lobster meat will shine regardless of its origin.*

*Chervil, also known as French parsley, is more delicate in flavor than regular curly or Italian parsley with a slight taste of licorice or aniseed. One-quarter cup fresh parsley plus 1/4 cup fresh tarragon can be substituted very successfully for the chervil in this recipe.*

# curry leaf *and* bacon hopping john

I ADORE CHEF LINTON HOPKINS and his establishments Holeman & Finch and the legendary Atlanta fine-dining institution, Restaurant Eugene. I call him Sir Hopkins—I revere this man so. He has taught me countless lessons on using the heirloom ingredients of our region. He has also led by example, showing how to introduce heritage produce into restaurant menus and, in the process, revive a unique ingredient and empower a small-shareholder farmer. His progressive thoughts on a work-life balance have been endlessly encouraging to me.

It was Sir Hopkins who introduced me to Carolina Gold rice. I'll always be grateful. This rice dubbed "the grandfather of American rice" has a fluffy, tender texture and a subtle sweetness. This grain, which has been grown since the 1600s along South Carolina and Georgia coastlands, was nearly lost. It went out of favor as hardier cultivars made their way into the market. The work of dedicated agricultural preservationists brought this special rice back into production. Seek out this rice: the flavor is unique, and the pearly grains have a luscious feel on the tongue.

On New Year's Day I cook these well-seasoned black-eyed peas and a batch of my Mess O' Greens (page 85) for prosperity and good luck—another addition to my new South traditions.

1 pound bacon, diced

1 teaspoon cumin seeds

1 teaspoon brown mustard seeds

6 fresh curry leaves

1 large yellow onion, diced

3 celery stalks, diced

2 medium red bell peppers, seeded and diced (about 1 cup)

2 serrano chiles, seeded and finely chopped

4 garlic cloves, finely chopped

1/2 teaspoon clove powder

1 teaspoon fresh coarsely ground black peppercorns

1 teaspoon kosher salt

1 pound dried black-eyed peas, rinsed and soaked overnight, then strained.

1 quart chicken stock

1/2 cup rice wine vinegar

3 green onions, thinly sliced, for garnish

3 cups cooked Carolina Gold Rice

Heat a large Dutch oven over moderate heat. Add the bacon and render until brown, about 6 to 8 minutes.

Add the cumin seeds and mustard seeds; toast until the mustard seeds pop, about 30 seconds. Add the curry leaves, onion, celery, bell pepper, and serrano chiles and cook, stirring occasionally, until the onion is translucent, about 5 to 6 minutes. Add the garlic and stir for another minute.

Add the clove powder, black pepper, and salt and stir well for another minute.

Add the black-eyed peas, the chicken stock, and the rice wine vinegar. Bring to a boil over high heat. Reduce the heat to low and cover the pot and cook until the peas are creamy and tender, about 45 minutes to an hour.

Garnish with green onions and serve over Carolina Gold Rice.

## CAROLINA GOLD RICE

1 cup Carolina Gold rice

1/2 teaspoon sea salt

2 teaspoons unsalted butter, cut into pieces

Rinse the rice with cold water until the water runs clear and drain through a fine mesh colander. Place the rice and 1 1/2 cups of water and salt in a deep, heavy-bottomed pot and cover. Place the pot over medium-low heat and allow it to come to a boil slowly. Reduce the heat and cook the rice for 14 minutes. It's best not to peek and allow the steam to escape. When the rice has finished cooking, the water should have been absorbed by the rice. Remove the pot from the heat and fluff the rice with a fork. Mix in unsalted butter and serve immediately.

# railways beef curry

ONE OF MY FONDEST FOOD memories of Kerala is traveling by train on the Southern Railway, which serves the culturally rich area known as India's Southern Peninsula. Because the railway caters to passengers rather than freight, a unique feature on the trains is a dining compartment featuring regional specialties. Additionally, at each station along the route, local vendors selling banana-leaf-wrapped curry dishes swaddled in newspaper meet trains and hungry travelers. I don't always remember where I traveled on the trains, but I have distinct memories of what I ate. This recipe is a re-creation of a fragrantly wrapped dish that remains vivid in my rec-ollections. It is similar to, but more nuanced than, traditional American beef stew. The ginger, garlic, and chiles in this dish pack a punch, and the coriander, garam masala, and cinnamon bark introduce beau-tiful complex flavors. The added perfume of the curry leaves is evocative of Kerala's aromatics.

Use a well-marbled piece of beef chuck to assure the dish is lip-lickingly succulent.

2 tablespoons canola oil

4 tablespoons coconut oil, divided

10 curry leaves

1 large red onion, thinly sliced

2 teaspoons kosher salt

2 tablespoons peeled, grated fresh ginger

2 teaspoons very finely chopped garlic

3 dried red chiles

2 sticks cinnamon

1 teaspoon cayenne pepper

1 teaspoon garam masala

1/2 teaspoon turmeric powder

1 tablespoon ground coriander

1 tablespoon sweet paprika

1 large tomato, peeled, seeded, and chopped (1 cup)

2 tablespoons tomato paste

3 pounds beef chuck, cut into 1-inch cubes

**MAKES 6 SERVINGS**

In a large skillet over medium-high heat, heat the canola oil and 2 tablespoons of the coconut oil until very hot. Add the curry leaves. The leaves will begin to sizzle in about 30 seconds. Add the onion and the salt and cook, stirring occasionally, until the onions soften, about 3 to 4 minutes. Add the ginger, garlic, chiles, and cinnamon sticks; stir for a minute, then add the cayenne, garam masala, turmeric, coriander, and paprika. Cook and stir for 2 minutes. Add the tomatoes and tomato paste and cook and stir until the tomatoes start releasing their juices, about 3 to 4 minutes.

Add the beef and increase the heat to high. Stir to coat the beef well with the sauce, and bring to a boil. Reduce the heat; cover and simmer until the beef is tender, about 45 minutes to 1 hour. When the beef is fully cooked, turn the heat to high and scrape all of the browned bits from the bottom of the pan, incorporating them into the beef and pan sauce. Add the remaining 2 tablespoons of coconut oil, stir, and serve immediately.

Although Christianity is the third-most practiced religion in India, the Christian population of Kerala is proportionately larger than in the rest of the nation. So for me, as a Christian, there were no taboos against eating beef in my household. In fact, tens of millions of people in India consume beef, although the slaughter of beef is only legal in a few states and buffalo is more common than beef. Any well-meaning hostess should consider any dietary requirements of her guests, often a matter of personal choice as opposed to some religious mandate.

# bright fruit salad topped *with* seasoned shrimp *and* cardamom honey lime dressing

GETTING TO KNOW MY PURVEYORS has been an added bonus in my culinary life. One of my favorites is Timmy Stubbs, a third-generation shrimper, who trolls the waters around Georgia's Jekyll and Tybee Islands, harvesting shrimp. He delivers to the Atlanta area twice a week. Timmy provides his impressive list of clients with an all-natural product devoid of preservatives. He flash-freezes his catch only if conditions prevent delivery within 48 hours. Timmy is a salt-of-the-earth kind of guy; there's nothing pretentious about him—just a fellow who takes a lot of pride in what he does for a living. He's a natural-born storyteller, and he'll sometimes wait around while I cook up the shrimp he brings me. Then the two of us will have lunch together and exchange childhood experiences and stories of growing up along our a-world-apart coasts.

Timmy's fresh, sweet shrimp combined with peppery arugula and ripe fruits drizzled with Cardamom Honey Lime Dressing is one of my favorite lunchtime offerings, in no small part due to my treasured visits from Timmy.

### SALAD

2 cups fresh watermelon, diced

1 cup peeled fresh papaya, seeded and diced

1 medium fresh mango, peeled and diced (1 cup)

1/2 cup yellow cherry tomatoes, cut in half

1/4 cup pomegranate seeds

1/2 pound baby arugula (about 6 cups)

1/2 cup Cardamom Honey Lime Dressing

### SEASONED SHRIMP

2 tablespoons olive oil

1 teaspoon garlic powder

1 teaspoon sweet paprika powder

1 teaspoon cayenne pepper powder

1 teaspoon kosher salt

1 pound shrimp (15 to 20 count), peeled and deveined

Place all the fruits, including the tomatoes and pomegranate seeds, in a large bowl and refrigerate to give the flavors a chance to mingle while you make the dressing and cook the shrimp.

In a medium skillet over medium-high heat, heat the olive oil and add the garlic powder, paprika, cayenne, and salt; stir and cook for 30 seconds. Toss in the shrimp and mix well to coat the shrimp in the spiced oil. Cook, stirring occasionally until the shrimp are just cooked through, about 2 to 3 minutes.

Add the arugula to the fruits and toss with the dressing. Place the shrimp on top of the salad and serve immediately.

### CARDAMOM HONEY LIME DRESSING

1/2 cup honey

1/4 cup freshly squeezed lime juice

1 teaspoon green cardamom powder

1/2 cup extra virgin olive oil

In a medium bowl, whisk the honey, lime juice, and cardamom together. Slowly drizzle the olive oil into the dressing, while constantly whisking, until the dressing is emulsified. Dressing may be stored refrigerated for up to two weeks.

# garam masala filé gumbo

I LOVE OKRA. It happens to be one of my favorite vegetables. In Kerala we have a dish that's made with prawns and okra and served over plain, piping hot white rice. Gumbo in many ways reminds me of that dish. In Louisiana, cooks use filé, a dark-green powder made from ground sassafras leaves, to thicken their gumbo. I learned about filé on travels down in Louisiana and soon became fond of its woodsy flavor notes. Make sure the gumbo does not boil after the filé powder is added. Overheating filé powder will cause it to become stringy or "thread," as they say down in Louisiana. Adding the spicy blend of garam masala to a shrimp gumbo and ladling up the luscious dish from a big pot to share with family and friends appeals to my South by South sense of community.

1/2 pound andouille sausage, cut into 1/4-inch pieces (see notes)

1/2 cup plus 2 tablespoons canola oil

1 cup unbleached all-purpose flour

1 tablespoon unsalted butter

1 large yellow onion, diced (about 1 cup)

4 celery stalks, diced

1 small green bell pepper, seeded and diced (about 1/2 cup)

2 small red bell peppers, seeded and diced (about 1 cup)

4 garlic cloves, finely chopped

2 medium Roma tomatoes, seeded and chopped

1 tablespoon kosher salt

1/2 teaspoon fresh coarsely ground black peppercorns

1 teaspoon garam masala

1 teaspoon green cardamom powder

1/2 teaspoon cayenne pepper

3 bay leaves

2 quarts shrimp stock (see notes)

1 1/2 pounds shrimp (16 to 20 count), peeled and deveined, reserving shells for stock

1 tablespoon filé powder

1/2 pound fresh okra (about eighteen 2- to 4-inch pods), halved lengthwise

4 cups cooked white long grain rice, for serving

**MAKES 8 SERVINGS**

Place a large cast-iron Dutch oven over medium heat. Add the sausage and cook until deeply browned, about 5 to 7 minutes. Remove and set aside.

Add the oil to the Dutch oven and sprinkle the flour over the oil; add the butter and cook over medium heat, stirring constantly and taking care to break up lumps of flour, until brown, about 10 minutes.

Gently add the onions, celery, peppers, and garlic and cook, stirring constantly until the onions begin to turn translucent, about 7 to 8 minutes. Add the tomatoes, salt, black pepper, garam masala, cardamom powder, cayenne pepper, and bay leaves and stir to combine. Gradually add the shrimp stock while whisking continuously.

Reduce the heat to low; cover and cook for 30 minutes. Add the shrimp and sausage and stir to combine. Cook, stirring frequently, for 5 to 6 minutes. Turn off the heat. Add the filé powder, stirring constantly. Cover and allow to sit for 10 minutes prior to serving.

In a medium sauté pan over high heat, add 2 tablespoons oil and fry the okra for about 5 minutes; remove from the oil and sprinkle with a pinch of salt and set aside.

Serve the gumbo in a bowl over steamed rice and top with okra.

**NOTES:** *In the US, andouille is a coarse-grained, doubled-smoked, Cajun-style spiced sausage traditionally made using pork shoulder or butt, garlic, pepper, onions, wine, and seasonings. In France, however, the meat ingredients of the sausage are generally derived from pig chitterlings and tripe. The Louisiana version is much spicier than its French counterpart. Several common commercial varieties are available in most grocery stores, as well as many artisan brands offered at butcher shops, farmers' markets, specialty groceries, and online.*

*I always make shrimp stock with shrimp shells, heads, or tails— whether the recipe calls for it or not. Generously cover the discarded parts with water in a large boiler, or stockpot, and add whatever cast-off trimmings of vegetables and herbs you have on hand. Lemon butts and rinds, celery and carrot trimmings, stems from herbs and onion, and garlic peels can all add flavor to shrimp stock. Toss in a bay leaf and some peppercorns and bring it all to a rolling boil. Let the mixture simmer until the liquid reduces by a third. Turn off the heat and set it aside to cool, then strain, leaving the solid pieces in the pot. The resulting aromatic and flavorful stock can be used either in the shrimp recipe you are making or frozen for later use in quick, savory seafood soups and chowders.*

# onion lentil dumplings
## *in* savory buttermilk

IN KERALA, *VADA* REFERS TO A SAVORY SNACK that takes the form of a type of dumpling or fritter. As often is the case in Indian cuisine, the dish takes on many different forms with varying shapes and ingredients. But the essence of any *vada* lies in the use of lentils as an ingredient. Of course, in America's deep southern states, dumplings are featured in many comfort foods, such as tomato gravy and dumplings and the classic chicken and dumplings. This recipe is *vada* reimagined, producing a new version of an old southern comfort food.

## BUTTERMILK BASE

4 cups high-quality buttermilk
(see notes)

1/2 teaspoon Kashmiri chili powder

1/2 teaspoon turmeric powder

1/2 teaspoon garam masala

1 1/2 teaspoons kosher salt

1/2 cup lentil flour

In a 4-quart bowl, combine the buttermilk, 1 cup of water, chili powder, turmeric powder, garam masala, salt, and lentil flour. Whisk until there are no lumps. Set mixture aside while preparing the dumplings.

**NOTES:** *Many health-food stores and specialty markets now carry premium buttermilk. Family farms such as Cruze Farm in east Tennessee are producing genuine old-fashioned buttermilk made the same way they did back in the day, beginning with the acidic, mostly defatted liquid left over from butter making. Premium buttermilk is pale yellow in color with flecks of butter still visible. It is worth seeking out premium brands for this recipe; you will notice a big difference in taste and texture. Also, look for Bulgarian-style buttermilk; it is thicker than some buttermilks and has a pronounced tang.*

## DUMPLINGS

1 cup lentil flour

1/2 teaspoon chili powder

1/2 teaspoon turmeric

1/2 teaspoon garam masala

1/2 teaspoon kosher salt

2 large yellow onions, halved and thinly sliced (about 1 1/2 cups)

Canola oil, for frying

In a large mixing bowl, combine the lentil flour with the chili powder, turmeric, garam masala, and salt. Add the onions and, using your hands, mix until the ingredients are well combined. Cover the bowl and let sit for 10 minutes, during which time the onions will release their juices into the flour mixture and moisten the batter. Add 2 tablespoons of water and stir to make a thick pound cake-like batter, adding a bit more water if needed.

In a large skillet, heat 2 inches of canola oil to 300°F. Drop tablespoons of the batter into the oil and fry for 2 minutes on each side. Fry in batches, being careful to not overcrowd, and lower the temperature of the oil. Drain dumplings on paper towel.

## ASSEMBLING THE DISH

2 tablespoons canola oil

1 teaspoon cumin seeds

1 medium white onion, thinly sliced

1 tablespoon peeled, finely chopped fresh ginger

1 tablespoon very finely chopped garlic

2 serrano green chile peppers, diced

In a heavy-bottomed stockpot, heat the canola oil over medium-low heat; add the cumin seeds and stir for 30 seconds. Add the onion and cook, stirring occasionally until the onion begins to soften, about 3 minutes. Add the ginger, garlic, and green chiles and cook and stir for 1 minute. Slowly add the buttermilk base, stirring well. Increase the heat to medium and bring to a boil. Stir often to keep the bottom from scorching. Reduce the heat to low and simmer the soup, stirring often, until the soup thickens to a gravy-like consistency, about 6 to 7 minutes. Add the dumplings to the soup, stir gently, and serve immediately.

# clove and ginger butternut squash soup

LIKE MANY PEOPLE, BUTTERNUT SQUASH MAKES ME THINK OF THE VIBRANT, WARM COLORS OF FALL. The scent of clove signals the beginning of cool weather. This creamy, fragrant soup is perfect for lunch on a brisk autumn day. During fall break, my son and I enjoy trips to our local farmers' market, where I enlist Ethan's help in picking out the ingredients. Back home, he helps me put it all together for our lunch. He loves a great soup, particularly if it's this hearty, nutritious bowl full of goodness. Preparing this recipe as a team is a great mother-son activity.

**MAKES 4 TO 6 SERVINGS**

2 tablespoons ghee

2 medium shallots, peeled and chopped

1 tablespoon peeled, finely chopped fresh ginger

1/2 teaspoon clove powder

1/2 teaspoon freshly ground black peppercorns

2 teaspoons kosher salt

1 medium butternut squash (2 pounds), peeled, seeded, and cut into 1-inch cubes (see notes)

3 cups vegetable stock

3 cups coconut milk

In a 4-quart pot over medium-high heat, heat the ghee. Add the shallots and cook, stirring occasionally, until the shallots are translucent, about 3 to 4 minutes. Add the ginger and stir for 1 minute, then add the clove powder, pepper, salt, squash, and stock. Bring to a simmer, and then reduce heat to medium low. Simmer until the squash is tender, about 20 minutes. Using an emulsion blender, purée the soup, or remove squash with a slotted spoon and transfer to a blender or food processor, purée, then return to the soup pot. Add the coconut milk and bring to a quick boil, then remove from heat. Serve hot.

**NOTES:** *A butternut squash can seem impenetrable. I use a cleaver to cut this hard-rind winter squash and occasionally have to place a hot pad over the top of the cleaver and give it a whack with a mallet to open the squash.*

*Baked mashed sweet potatoes are an easy, tasty substitution for the butternut squash in this soup.*

# pickled catfish

Thus far, the highlight of my culinary career was the day John T. Edge, the acclaimed culinary author and academic, invited me to cook a luncheon for a Southern Foodways Alliance Symposium. Leading up to the event, I was a ball of nerves, so I decided to do an advance test run at the Alliance home located at the Center for the Study of Southern Culture at the University of Mississippi. Preparing for my trip to Oxford, I wanted to present John T. with a gift that reflected the culinary traditions of both my Souths. I sought a way to pay homage to the Southern Foodways Alliance, while also presenting a little bit of my heritage and background. While living in the American South, I'd been exposed to the great tradition of pickling vegetables and fruits such as okra and watermelon rind. Similarly, my native land of Kerala, a coastal seafaring region, had a long tradition of preserving fish. When the sea was abundant, the fishing communities would take care to pickle and dry fish ahead of the monsoons. When the rains came and the sea was too rough for the fishermen, the pickled, preserved fish provided delicious sustenance. My mother always chose a firm fish, like kingfish (mackerel), that held up to the pickling brine of vinegar, salt, and Kerala spices. In considering John T.'s realm, I naturally hit upon that delicious staple of the South, catfish. It is a moist, firm fish with a consistently mild, sweet taste that absorbs spices and other flavors well. I had settled on my gift—pickled catfish!

A farm-raised catfish is preserved in an *escabeche*-like preparation; a method that uses an acidic marinade mixture that harkens back to the Portuguese influence on my coastal Indian heritage. My preserved catfish recipe progressed from a gift idea to a signature dish as it evolved via batches and batches and the intermingling of fond flavors and friends.

I like to serve pickled catfish at room temperature on top of a big salad for lunch or over piping hot rice for a heartier meal.

2 pounds US farm-raised catfish fillets, cut into 2-inch pieces (see notes)

1 teaspoon turmeric powder

1 teaspoon freshly ground black peppercorns

2 teaspoons kosher salt, divided

2 cups canola oil

4 tablespoons mustard oil (see notes)

1 teaspoon brown mustard seeds

1/2 cup peeled, finely chopped fresh ginger

1 tablespoon hot paprika

1 teaspoon cayenne powder

1/2 teaspoon asafoetida powder

1 teaspoon white granulated sugar

2 teaspoons kosher salt, divided

1 cup rice wine vinegar

Combine the catfish, turmeric, pepper, and 1 teaspoon of salt and set aside for 30 minutes.

In a deep skillet, heat the canola oil to 275°F. Fry the seasoned fish until golden brown, about 2 minutes. Set the fish on a paper-towel-lined plate to drain. Remove the oil from the skillet.

Heat the skillet over medium-high heat; add the mustard oil and mustard seeds, and toast seeds until they pop, about 30 seconds. Reduce the heat to medium low; add the ginger and cook, stirring, until the ginger is golden brown, about 3 to 4 minutes. Add the paprika, cayenne, asafoetida, sugar, and the remaining teaspoon of salt and cook for 1 minute. Add the vinegar and reduce the heat to low and simmer until thickened, about 5 minutes. Remove the skillet from the heat and add the catfish and coat the fish with the sauce. Let the catfish cool in the sauce. When the fish is cool, place it in two mason jars and divide the sauce between the jars. Seal and refrigerate the fish for at least 24 hours and up to two weeks.

Allow fish to come to room temperature before serving.

**NOTES:** *First off, use good US farm-raised catfish. Always demand to know where your catfish comes from. Simmons Farm Raised Catfish in Mississippi has a prime cut named Delacata that is just right for this recipe. The Simmons family has been farming catfish in the artesian aquifers of the Mississippi Delta since 1982, and they are now a third-generation family business.*

*Look for pungent mustard oil in Indian markets, larger natural food stores, or online. It is a nice addition to vinaigrettes. Mustard oil is pressed from field mustard and rape, two plants that are closely related to black mustard.*

# summer green bean *and* corn salad

I LOVE FISH SAUCE. The Thai and Korean varieties are particular favorites. I'm lucky to have a kitchen that on some days will allow me to play around with an ingredient over which I have been obsessing. I discovered that fish sauce can be an amazing base for a vinaigrette. Lime, honey, and olive oil whisked with the slightly funky qualities of this Asian condiment and served over freshly shucked corn and crunchy green beans make for a salad I could eat every day during a summer season of tender sweet corn and velvet-skinned, freshly picked pole beans. The dressing works wonderfully later in the summer drizzled over steamed yellow squash.

**MAKES 6 SERVINGS**

2 pounds fresh green beans, trimmed

1 teaspoon kosher salt

Ice bath, for green beans

1/4 cup Thai fish sauce

1/4 cup lime juice

Zest of 2 limes

1/4 cup honey

1/4 cup extra virgin olive oil

1 cup fresh corn kernels (about 2 large ears)

In a 3-quart saucepan, bring 2 quarts of water and the salt to a boil and place the green beans in for 5 minutes; drain the water out and place the beans in your ice bath (large bowl of water with ice). Drain the beans and set aside in the fridge to cool.

In a small bowl, whisk together the fish sauce, lime juice and zest, and honey. Slowly drizzle the olive oil into the dressing, while constantly whisking, until the dressing is emulsified. Add the shucked corn to the beans. Pour the dressing over the salad, toss, and serve.

# red quinoa *and* avocado grain bowl

SPICE TO TABLE, MY LITTLE PATISSERIE, is located in an Atlanta neighborhood with a vegetarian-friendly demographic. The Old Fourth Ward neighborhood, called by the *New York Times* "a cradle of culinary innovation," is home to The King Center, Ebenezer Baptist Church, Inman Park, and the Atlanta Civic Center. This friendly neighborhood is quite diverse and attracts all types of diners. We regularly change our salad menu based on what is fresh and seasonally available to satisfy our customers' desire for healthy, wholesome ingredients.

As part of my work as a CARE chef ambassador, I have been fortunate to be exposed to many foods that I never knew existed. Many are plant based and have adapted well to the Spice to Table menu. On one CARE trip to Peru, I met a farmer named Soto who introduced me to delectable red quinoa.

Soto is a proud person, a man of the earth who managed to continue farming through years of civil war. He's a farmer who kept trying to salvage the native traditions of his home even after the war, but the market did not reward him. One look at his hands told me the story of his whole life—his pride as a farmer, his connection to the land, and his endless hard work. With those rugged hands, he grows products that are the legacy of his ancestors. Yet finding a market for his grain was very difficult. Things began looking up for Soto, however, when he learned that CARE was assisting local farmers to boost production and link them with reliable markets in Lima and beyond. The project offered high-quality seeds and helped organize the farmers into a cooperative. Today, Soto and his consortium partners are earning a livable, sustainable income. The takeaway here is that when consumers make room in their lives for heritage produce, it can make a world of difference to farmers like Soto.

Quinoa is quick cooking and gluten free. It is often referred to and cooked as a grain. In actuality, it is a pseudograin, the seed of a beet relative. This nutritious food comes in a variety of colors, the most common being white, red, and black. Red quinoa has a crunchier texture than the white variety and tends to be less sticky. By adding this Red Quinoa and Avocado Grain Bowl into our restaurant menu rotation, we discovered a customer favorite while also helping to sustain farmers like Soto.

2 tablespoons canola oil

1 teaspoon cumin seeds

1 shallot, peeled and finely chopped

1/4 cup golden raisins

1 cup red quinoa, rinsed

Zest of 2 lemons

Juice of 1 lemon

1 teaspoon white granulated sugar

1 teaspoon kosher salt

2 avocados, peeled, pitted, and sliced

1/4 cup fresh dill, chopped

Heat the canola oil in a 2-quart saucepan over medium heat. Add the cumin seeds and stir for 30 seconds. Add the shallots and cook, stirring occasionally, until they are translucent, about 4 minutes. Stir in the raisins. Add the quinoa, 2½ cups of water, lemon zest and juice, sugar, and salt. Bring the quinoa to a boil, then cover and reduce heat to low. Simmer for 20 minutes, or until the quinoa is tender. Fluff with a fork. Transfer the quinoa to a serving bowl and gently toss in the avocado and fresh dill.

# cooling yogurt rice

JANUARY THROUGH JUNE IS SWELTERING IN KERALA, often 98 degrees in the shade. As a youngster, I'd rush home for lunch from school hot and hungry, asking my mom, "What's to eat?" Invariably any number of spice-forward snacks and dishes were offered, ready for immediate consumption. But in a remote, shaded corner of the kitchen, I knew my mother always kept an earthenware pot of cool yogurt rice, a refreshing way to quell the heat inside and provide relief from the heat outside. I have a similar crock on my counter most summer afternoons for my on-the-go tween and his posse.

**MAKES 6 SERVINGS**

1 cup white basmati rice

2 teaspoons kosher salt, divided

3 tablespoons olive oil

1 teaspoon brown mustard seeds

1 tablespoon peeled, finely chopped fresh ginger

3 whole dried red chiles

2 cups (16 ounces) plain whole Greek-style yogurt

In a medium pot, place the rice, 2 cups of water, and 1 teaspoon of the salt. Bring the water to a rolling boil over high heat. Lower the heat to the lowest setting, cover the pot with a tight-fitting lid, and cook for 12 minutes.

Meanwhile, heat the oil in a large skillet over medium heat; add the mustard seeds and stir until the seeds pop, about 30 seconds. Add the ginger and chiles and cook, stirring, for 1 minute. Add the yogurt and remaining teaspoon of salt. Stir well then remove from the heat.

When the rice has finished cooking, fluff it with a fork and then add it to the seasoned yogurt. Serve right away or at room temperature. This is best eaten the day it is made. Over time, the rice-yogurt mixture will thicken to a custard-like texture.

# tea times & party

# times

*At Carmel Compound, my family's home in Kerala, we never knew who would come calling to pay a visit. Whether invited or unannounced, guests were always considered a blessing, and when they came, it was expected that you serve food and refreshments.*

This was and still is simply part of the Indian culture. Because of this tradition, my mother always made sure she had copious cauldrons of chai, the spiced, milky black tea renowned as our national beverage, warm and ready. Served hot, chai is perfect for piquing the body's natural cooling reflexes and therefore was a considerate beverage choice to offer visitors coming in from the sweltering heat to rest and visit. My aunts always had a variety of snacks prepared for afternoon callers and took pride in their creations.

During my early teenage years, dating frequently consisted simply of "cutting chai."

Young couples shared a half glass of the beverage from a street vendor or at a café. Sadly, today's teens in India are more often opting for coffee shops and bonding over what Americans call a "cuppa joe." Yet the importance of chai as an integral part of social mores remains throughout India. The social aspect of chai may have predisposed me to open Third Space and Spice to Table. Here in my American hometown, people drop by these two establishments to say hello and Tea Time often segues into Happy Hour.

# asha's chai

MY FAVORITE VESSEL FOR DRINKING CHAI is a slightly dinged-up, pale-blue, porcelain-enameled metal mug. It has spots of dark, aged metal showing around the rim and handle. It is my favorite because it reminds me of my great-aunt. For me tea time is a bit sweeter with this vintage cup warming my hands and filling my head with steamy spicy scents. Sweeten to your liking.

**MAKES 4 SERVINGS**

2 cups whole milk

8 green cardamom pods, crushed

1/4 teaspoon freshly grated nutmeg

1/2 teaspoon ginger powder

4 tablespoons black Assam tea leaves (see notes)

In a 2-quart pot over very low heat, heat the milk and 2 cups of water with the cardamom, nutmeg, and ginger until the liquid is infused with the spices, about 20 minutes.

Add the tea leaves, and over high heat simmer for 1 minute, keeping a close eye to make sure it does not boil over.

Remove the tea from the heat and let the tea leaves steep for 3 to 4 minutes. Strain and serve piping hot.

**NOTES:** *Assam tea is a black, full-bodied tea produced in the Assam region in India; it lies on either side of the Brahmaputra River, which borders Bangladesh and Burma. This tea is known for its strong, bright color and distinctive brisk, malty flavor. Many teas sold as "breakfast tea" contain Assam tea.*

# arabian sweet tea

WHILE CHAI IS CONSIDERED THE NATIONAL DRINK OF INDIA, I, like folks in the American South, also love ice-cold sweet tea as a treat in the late afternoon. This tea is mint-muddled and magnificently aromatic, a recipe often enjoyed in the tea salons and cafés along the Arabian Sea's coast.

**MAKES 4 SERVINGS**

3 tablespoons white granulated sugar

4 teaspoons Darjeeling tea leaves (see notes)

2 (about 2 x 2-inch) pieces orange rind (only the colored rind, not the white pith)

½ cup fresh mint leaves plus mint sprigs for garnish

In a 2-quart pot, boil 4 cups of water. Add the sugar and stir until dissolved. Remove the sugar water from the heat. Drop the tea leaves, orange rind, and mint leaves into the sugar water and steep for about 5 minutes. Strain, then chill the tea before serving over ice. Garnish with fresh mint sprigs, if desired.

**NOTES:** *Fine Darjeeling tea is cultivated at altitudes of about seven thousand feet in the Himalayan foothills of Darjeeling province in West Bengal, India. It is thin-bodied with a light color, and its flavor characteristics are sometimes described as floral with a pleasant hint of tannin, reminiscent of the properties of the Muscat grape. It brews to a pale golden color and is perfect for serving cold.*

# sparkling midnight thyme rosé

THIS SPARKLING DRINK IS A GREAT WAY TO RING IN A MIDNIGHT CELEBRATION of a birthday, an anniversary, or a New Year. Sparkling rosé is growing in popularity around the globe. Don't let the pinkish hue fool you; rosé wines commonly have an alcohol content over 12 percent. Red grapes tint these bubbly wines, which have a bright flavor that is not overpowered by the herbed syrup.

**MAKES 6 COCKTAILS**

6 teaspoons rosewater (see notes)

6 tablespoons Thyme-Infused Syrup, chilled

1 (75 liter) bottle chilled dry sparkling rosé (I like to use Spumante Brut Rosé)

6 edible rose petals

6 tender sprigs fresh thyme

In each champagne flute, pour 1 teaspoon of rosewater and 1 tablespoon of Thyme-Infused Syrup. Top off with the sparkling rosé and give it a quick swirl. Garnish with a rose petal and a sprig of thyme.

**NOTES:** *Rosewater is water that has been steam distilled with fresh rose petals. Be sure the rosewater is all natural and not made with a synthetic rose oil. A quick online search will yield several step-by-step video tutorials for making rosewater in your home kitchen.*

## THYME-INFUSED SYRUP

1 cup white granulated sugar

10 sprigs fresh thyme

In a small pot, bring 1 cup of water to a boil over high heat, add sugar, and stir until the sugar has dissolved. Add the thyme and let it infuse in the syrup for 15 minutes. Strain and chill the syrup.

# warm sorghum toddy

IN INDIA, TODDY IS THE NAME OF A TYPE OF LIQUOR derived from the sap of several species of the palm tree, including Palmyra, date, and coconut palms. The name comes from an English distortion of *tari*, the Hindi word for palm sap. Toddy is still made in homes and consumed in Kerala. In the American South, people regularly enjoy a hot toddy that, while being a long way from the traditional version, owes at least its name to my first South. In this recipe, bourbon is sweetened with a warm concoction of sorghum and spiced apple cider; spinning a cinnamon stick through it all produces a heady vapor that takes the chill out of your bones.

**MAKES 4 DRINKS**

½ cup sorghum syrup (see notes)

4 cups apple cider

6 star anise

2 cinnamon sticks plus 4 for garnish

8 ounces bourbon

In a 2-quart pot over medium heat, bring the sorghum syrup, cider, star anise, and cinnamon to a boil. Reduce the heat to low and simmer for 20 minutes, or until reduced by one-third. Strain the spiced cider into four mugs. Add 2 ounces of bourbon to each cup and stir. Serve warm with a cinnamon stick garnish, if desired.

**NOTES:** *Sorghum syrup is derived from tall-growing, bicolor sorghum grass (Andropogon saccharatus), which features long stems, flat leaves, and a small feathery seed head. Sweet sorghum is naturally high in sugar content, unlike some cultivars grown for grain and fodder. This variety is grown specifically for the production of syrup and is chiefly found in the southeastern United States, most notably in Tennessee and Kentucky. Look for 100 percent pure sorghum syrup at farm stands, specialty markets, or online. Unlike true molasses, which is made as a by-product of sugarcane or sugar beet sugar extraction, sorghum syrup has a buttery complexity.*

BOURBON IS AN AMERICAN WHISKEY primarily made from corn and aged in new, charred white oak barrels. Although its origin is subject to much controversy, some people assume it is rooted in Bourbon County, Kentucky—although few outside that area give that version credence. Though most origin stories are impossible to verify, one fact is clear and mandated by law—*bourbon whiskey* is a distinctive product of the United States. Although it can be produced anywhere it is legal to distill, most popular bourbon brands are still associated with Kentucky (neighboring Tennessee prefers to distinguish its bourbon products as Tennessee whiskey). To qualify as true straight bourbon, the mash used in distillation must consist of at least 51 percent but not more than 79 percent corn, aged for at least two years in oak barrels. Another stipulation is only water can be added to lower the alcohol content, which is commonly 80 proof—although 86, 90, and 100 proofs are available. Barrel proof or undiluted bourbon can go as high as 160 proof. Although any bourbon, rye whiskey, Irish whiskey, or scotch can be substituted in this recipe, I have come to believe that only *real* bourbon from the southern United States renders the most delicious results!

# spicy cold old monk

My *achan* (father) was a whiskey lover: Johnnie Walker in all his colors—red, black, green, blue—graced my father's whiskey collection. But among them there always sat that bottle of Old Monk Rum. This dark rum is a staple in many Indian households, from officers in the Indian armed forces to the common man on the street. Old Monk Rum has woven itself into the fabric of India, and when paired with Ginger Coffee (page 55) frozen into globes, it makes the perfect after-dinner drink.

1 cup Ginger Coffee (page 55), frozen into 2½-inch spheres (see notes)

8 ounces Old Monk Rum or other dark rum

Set up four thick-bottomed glass tumblers. Drop a single coffee ice sphere in each glass and pour 2 ounces of rum over each sphere. Sip and savor!

**NOTES:** *Ice ball molds made of silicone are available at many houseware shops and liquor stores and online. The beautiful shape melts slowly into the dark rum.*

# puff pastry samosa pockets *with* sirloin *and* sweet pea filling, curry chicken filling, *or* mango *and* jaggery filling

WHEN I OPENED MY DAYTIME DINING SPOT, SPICE TO TABLE, I wanted it to have a Southern sensibility while at the same time featuring strong Indian flavors. One of the first recipes I developed for my new endeavor was this variation of a traditional samosa, a fried pastry with a savory filling. I decided to use baked puff pastry instead of wrapping the filling in *madia* (wheat) flour and frying. The filling was kept pretty traditional with spicy coriander, black pepper, ground sirloin, and sweet peas. With the addition of jalapeño peppers and a bit of fresh cilantro to bring a bright pop of flavor to the filling, the resulting samosa pocket is a winner!

My dear mother was masterful at turning leftovers into tea-time treats. Besides the sweeter offerings, she sometimes whipped up small tasty bundles of savory bits from earlier meals encased in pastry. The recipe for this snack includes a chicken curry filling spiced with ginger, garam masala, and onions. The masala mixture can successfully be stirred into leftovers ranging from rotisserie chicken to roasted cauliflower. You, too, will become a master of the afternoon tea-time snack.

Also included here is a much requested brunch version—a sweet mango and jaggery filling with cumin.

## SIRLOIN and SWEET PEA FILLING

2 tablespoons canola oil

1 medium shallot, peeled and finely chopped

3 jalapeño peppers, seeded and finely chopped

2 teaspoons garlic powder

1 teaspoon fresh coarsely ground black peppercorns

2 teaspoons coriander powder

1/2 teaspoon turmeric powder

1 teaspoon kosher salt

1 pound ground sirloin

1/2 cup fresh or frozen green peas

1/2 cup cilantro leaves, chopped

MAKES 6 SAMOSAS

In a medium skillet, over medium heat, heat the oil until it starts to shimmer. Add the shallot and the jalapeño peppers and cook, stirring occasionally until the shallot begin to brown, about 5 minutes. Add the garlic powder, black pepper, coriander, turmeric, and salt and continue to cook, stirring, for 1 minute. Add the sirloin and peas and cook, stirring often until the beef is cooked and most of the juices have evaporated, about 8 minutes. Add the cilantro and remove from heat. Set aside to cool and fill the samosa pockets.

## CURRY CHICKEN FILLING

4 tablespoons canola oil

1 large yellow onion, thinly sliced

1 tablespoon peeled, finely chopped fresh ginger

2 teaspoons finely chopped garlic

1 tablespoon sweet paprika

1 1/2 teaspoons garam masala

1 tablespoon tomato paste

1 teaspoon kosher salt

1 pound boneless, skinless chicken breast, cut into 1/2-inch pieces

MAKES 6 SAMOSAS

In a medium skillet, over medium heat, heat the oil until it starts to shimmer. Add the onion and cook until it is a golden brown, about 4 to 5 minutes. Add the ginger and cook for another minute, stirring constantly. Add the garlic, paprika, garam masala, tomato paste, and salt along with 1/4 cup of water. Mix well until all the ingredients are incorporated. Simmer this sauce for another 2 minutes before adding the chicken. Cook for about 8 minutes, stirring often, until the chicken is cooked through. The liquids should all be evaporated at this point. Set aside to cool.

Transfer the chicken to a food processor and pulse about four to five times. Remove from food processor and fill the samosa pockets.

## MANGO and JAGGERY FILLING

3 tablespoons unsalted butter

3 tablespoons shaved jaggery

1/2 teaspoon cumin seeds

2 1/2 cups fresh or frozen mango, cut into 1/4-inch pieces

In a medium skillet over medium heat, melt the butter and jaggery; add the cumin and mangoes and cook for 8 to 10 minutes until the liquids have evaporated and the mangoes are glossy and coated with the jaggery. Set aside to cool and fill the samosa pockets.

## PUFF PASTRY

1 egg, beaten

1 tablespoon whole milk

1 (14 by 9-inch) sheet frozen puff pastry (two 14-ounce packages), thawed (see notes)

Heat the oven to 400°F. Line a large baking sheet with parchment paper. In a small bowl, whisk the egg and milk together to make an egg wash and set aside.

Cut six 4 1/2 x 4 1/2-inch squares of dough. Place about 1 1/2 heaping tablespoons of filling on the bottom half of each square of dough. Fold the dough over the filling, gently pressing out any air pockets, and then crimp the edges closed with a fork.

Place the samosas 2 inches apart on the baking sheet. Brush each samosa with the egg wash.

Bake the samosas until puffed and brown, about 15 minutes.

**NOTES:** *Look for ready-made puff pastry in the freezer section, particularly those brands made with all butter rather than oil. They will have a richer flavor, and the dough will produce nice layers of pastry.*

*Pop the completed samosas into the freezer for a few minutes before baking to firm up the butter. The chilled butter will melt slowly, producing steam as the pockets bake, which makes a crisp, even pastry rather than a lopsided and mushy one.*

# sweet potato *and* spinach bhajia *with* south *by* south's sweet *and* sour sauce

*BHAJIA*, OR PAKORA, are India's version of fritters. They are ubiquitous at tea time. At one point, I thought I had seen every vegetable possible turned into this ever-present afternoon snack. Then one day it occurred to me, I'd never seen *bhajia* made with the famous sweet potatoes of the American South. I found that the sweet potatoes, combined with fresh spinach, cumin, and red chili powder, bind nicely with lentil flour and fry to a savory crisp. Forming the fritters with a small hole in the center ensures the sweet potato dough cooks through completely. The sweet and sour aspect of tamarind adds a unique touch to many dishes, and it is a central ingredient in Worcestershire sauce. Here, I bring the sour of the tamarind, the sweetness of the sweet potatoes, and the mineral aspects of the spinach into a two-bite wonder.

1½ cups lentil flour

1 teaspoon cumin powder

½ teaspoon Kashmiri chili powder

½ teaspoon turmeric powder

½ teaspoon kosher salt

2 pounds sweet potatoes, grated

1 pound fresh spinach, roughly chopped

1 tablespoon canola oil plus more for frying

**MAKES 14 FRITTERS**

In a large bowl, combine the lentil flour, cumin, chili powder, turmeric, and salt. Using your hands, toss the sweet potatoes and spinach with 1 tablespoon of canola oil. Combine the sweet potato and spinach mixture with the lentil flour and spice mixture. Gradually add about 4 tablespoons of water to make a moldable, shapeable mass.

In a large, deep skillet, heat 1 inch of oil over medium heat to 300°F. Line a large baking sheet with paper towels for draining the fritters and set it aside. With slightly wet hands, take about 1½ tablespoons of the sweet potato mixture and mold it into a round shape in the palm of your hand. Using your index finger, make a hole in the center of each fritter and drop it in the oil. Fry the fritters for 2 minutes on each side, or until deep golden brown; work in batches so as not to crowd the skillet. Remove the fritters from the oil, allowing excess oil to drain into the skillet, then place the fritters on the paper-towel-lined baking sheet. Serve the fritters warm with South by South's Sweet and Sour Sauce.

# SOUTH *by* SOUTH'S SWEET *and* SOUR SAUCE

TAMARIND AND CANE SYRUP. Two iconic ingredients of my Souths hit with coarsely ground cumin and salt make this sauce a bridge for international snacking. The sauce keeps well in the refrigerator for two weeks. Keep it on hand for delicious dipping of all types of fried snacks, such as hushpuppies, onion rings, or chicken wings, giving them a whole new direction.

MAKES ABOUT 1 CUP

1½ cups water

2 tablespoons tamarind concentrate

2 teaspoons coarsely ground cumin

6 tablespoons cane syrup

1 teaspoon kosher salt

In a small saucepan over low flame, combine all of the ingredients. Stir well, making sure the tamarind concentrate is well incorporated. Simmer for 20 minutes, or until the sauce is reduced by one-third. Serve sauce at room temperature.

# fried green tomato delights

ALMOST EVERY CHEF IN ATLANTA HAS A VERSION OF FRIED GREEN TOMATOES on the menu. So, to keep up with and hopefully surpass the competition, I had to create an Asha version. Fried Green Tomato Delights feature golden turmeric, chickpea flour, shallots, and cumin with a dash of cayenne as a flourish. They are a distinctly southern Indian take on an iconic southern American staple. A cooking tip: be sure to mix the tomatoes into the seasoned flour just before you are ready to fry them up. If the mixture sits too long, the tomatoes release their liquid and the batter can be compromised.

Try these tomato snacks dunked in South by South's Sweet and Sour Sauce (page 132).

**MAKES 16 FRITTERS**

1 pound green tomatoes, seeded, halved crosswise, and thinly sliced

1 cup chickpea flour

½ cup rice flour

1 teaspoon cumin seeds, coarsely ground

1 teaspoon Kashmiri chili powder

1 teaspoon turmeric powder

1 teaspoon kosher salt

3 medium shallots, peeled and thinly sliced

Canola oil, for frying

Drain the tomatoes in a colander over a bowl for 30 minutes.

In a large bowl combine the chickpea flour, rice flour, cumin, Kashmiri chili powder, turmeric, and salt.

In a large deep skillet, heat 2 inches of oil over medium heat to 350°F. Line a plate with paper towels and set aside.

When ready to fry, add the tomatoes and shallots to the dry ingredients and mix well, thoroughly coating the vegetables. There is enough liquid in the tomatoes, so do not add any liquid. Working in batches of four, fry heaping tablespoons of the battered tomatoes, 2 minutes on each side until deep golden. Remove the fritters, allowing excess oil to drip into the skillet. Drain the fritters on the paper-towel-lined plate.

# carrot *and* mint chutney toast

EVEN THOUGH TEA-TIME ENTERTAINING WAS PREVALENT IN INDIA when I was growing up in the 1970s, the custom waned a bit with the advent of instant electronic communication. Fortunately, it seems to be making a comeback. The ladies are once again getting together to visit and showcase their cooking skills. As before, children are always invited. These crunchy, carrot-topped toasts continue to be a favorite finger food for my little friends and me. When entertaining, I set out one tray of these delightful toast snacks, already assembled. I also provide other trays of toast with all the fixings and let my guests assemble subsequent rounds. Such tactics serve two purposes: everything stays crisp, and everyone has fun and enjoys getting hands-on with their own combinations.

**MAKES 24 SERVINGS**

12 slices fresh (not frozen) Texas toast, any brand, crust trimmed and cut in half lengthwise

1 cup grated fresh carrots

1/2 cup Mint Chutney (page 90)

Canola oil, for frying

In a deep skillet over medium heat, heat 1 inch of oil to 350°F. Line a tray with paper towels and set aside.

Fry the bread slices a couple at a time for 1 minute on each side, or until crisp and light golden brown. Remove the toast from the oil, allowing the excess oil to drip into the skillet. Drain the toast on the paper towels.

Spread a thin layer of the chutney on top of each toast and top with the grated carrot. Serve at once.

**NOTES:** *Using the fried toast as a base, try different combinations of spreads and fresh toppings: salted butter and radishes, cashew butter with pears, or quince paste and manchego cheese.*

# radish *and* cucumber tea sandwiches

WHEN I MOVED TO ATLANTA, I soon learned the cultural and historical role of tea sandwiches. Sometimes referred to as finger sandwiches, the name suggests the long, narrow length of a dainty digit. Tea sandwiches are often cut in a triangular shape or in a small, biscuit-like round. For extra flare, a hostess may cleverly fashion her sandwiches with shaped cookie cutters. Regardless of their shape, a tea sandwich should show no hint of a crust, have minimal but tasty fillings, and be eaten in two delicate, ladylike bites. Third Space has quickly become a favored venue for showers and celebrations. Not surprisingly, one of our most requested afternoon offerings are these easy, make-ahead, satisfying sandwiches. Use a mandoline, or V-slicer, to slice the radishes and cucumbers into thin, uniform slices. Soak the radishes in ice water to give them a slightly milder taste and crisper crunch. Blot any excess moisture off of the radishes and cucumbers before assembling the sandwiches. Use the best quality butter and bread available as the delicate balance between the sharpness of the radish, the heat of the white pepper, and the clean, crisp flavor of the cucumber depends on these two simple ingredients.

4 radishes, washed, trimmed, and thinly sliced

Ice bath, for radishes

4 tablespoons (1/2 stick) top-quality salted butter, at room temperature

12 thin slices best-quality white bread

1 English cucumber, peeled and thinly sliced

1 teaspoon white pepper, divided

1/2 teaspoon kosher salt, divided

Place the sliced radishes in a bowl of ice water for 10 minutes, then drain and lay out on a towel to dry. Lightly butter one side of each of the twelve bread slices. Arrange a double layer of cucumber slices with the rounds slightly overlapping on six slices of the buttered bread. Sprinkle the cucumbers with 1/2 of the white pepper and 1/2 of the salt. Arrange the radishes over the cucumber slices and sprinkle with the remaining white pepper and salt.

Top the sandwiches with the six remaining slices of buttered bread. Using a serrated knife, and pressing down firmly, neatly cut the crusts from the sandwiches. Cut each sandwich into four individual tea sandwiches. Make the three cuts vertically across the bread for finger sandwiches or diagonally for triangular-shaped sandwiches. Serve immediately.

**NOTES:** *If the sandwiches must be made a little ahead of time and held until serving time, place a single layer of sandwiches in a lidded rectangular plastic or glass container. Cover the sandwiches loosely with a layer of waxed paper. Then put a slightly damp paper towel on top of the waxed paper; never put the wet towel directly on top of the sandwiches. Lastly, put the cover on the container and place it in the refrigerator. When ready to use, take the sandwiches from the refrigerator about an hour before they will be served and remove the container lid. Do not remove the towel or the waxed paper until ready to serve the sandwiches.*

# golden potato croquettes
## *or* aloo tikki

LIKE MOST OF THE WORLD, India has an abiding love of potatoes. This universal mainstay shows up in every conceivable shape all over the country from north to south and east to west. *Aloo tikki* always seems to make the list of tea-time favorites. *Aloo* means potato, and *tikki* is a small cutlet or croquet. Variations of this baked potato cake appear all over India; *aloo tikki* patties might be served sandwich-style between two pieces of bread, perched atop curried chickpeas, or crusted in lentil flour and fried crisp. Spiced with *ajowan* seeds, these little golden discs are a staple at Spice to Table. Our regular customers might organize a rebellion if these perfect bites of potato goodness were removed from our menu. Be sure to wear gloves and an apron to prevent your fingers and clothes from being stained yellow during the mixing and shaping of *aloo tikki*.

These savory snacks are nice served with Mint Chutney (page 90).

Nonstick cooking spray, for
parchment paper

4 tablespoons canola oil

1 large yellow onion, finely chopped

1 teaspoon turmeric powder

1 teaspoon cumin seeds

1 teaspoon ajowan seeds (see notes)

1 1/2 teaspoons kosher salt

1 teaspoon garlic powder

2 pounds gold potatoes, peeled,
boiled, and roughly mashed

2/3 cup chopped cilantro leaves
and stems

Heat the oven to 400°F. Line a large sheet pan with parchment paper and spray with nonstick cooking spray.

In a medium skillet over medium heat, heat the oil and add the onion. Cook and stir until the onion is translucent, about 3 to 4 minutes. Add the turmeric powder, cumin seeds, *ajowan* seeds, and salt. Cook and stir for 1 minute. Add the garlic powder; stir and remove from the heat. Let mixture stand to cool and blend flavors for about 10 minutes.

In a large mixing bowl, using gloved hands, combine the potatoes with the spiced onion mixture and cilantro. Form 12 small patties. Place the patties 2 inches apart on the sprayed parchment-paper-lined sheet pan and bake until a nice, slightly golden crust forms, about 15 minutes. Allow to cool for at least 5 minutes and serve.

**NOTES**: *Ajowan or ajwain seeds are also known as Bishop's weed. The tiny, pale seeds look similar to but taste nothing like cumin seeds. Rather, ajowan tastes like a stronger, more pungent variation of thyme mixed with notes of aniseed and oregano. Substitute oregano if ajowan seeds are not at hand or readily available for purchase. (It can often be found under different names or spellings, depending on the style of cuisine: ajave, ajowan, ajwan, aivain, aiwan, carom, Ethiopian cumin, oman, omum.) The unique flavor makes this spice well worth seeking out. Use it sparingly, as the seeds can easily come to dominate the flavor of a dish. Ajowan is also used as a medicinal herb; the seeds can be chewed to aid digestion.*

# black salt *and* pepper roasted cashews

ALTHOUGH IN KERALA, AS WELL AS IN INDIA GENERALLY, hospitality is a cultural mandate, in the American South, hospitality seems to run in people's DNA. Why, in many southern states, there is even a Miss Hospitality contest! In both my two Souths, hosts are never without a nibble to offer guests, but in the American South, it's usually offered with a highball. One such munchie I like to keep on hand to accompany libations are these addicting cashews. If anyone is around while you are making these, do your best to fend them off—because they won't last long otherwise! If you can accomplish this, a stockpile of these keeps well in an airtight container in the freezer for up to six months. I use *kala namak*, or Himalayan black salt, to flavor these cashews. A true rock salt, "black" salt is a bit of a misnomer in that, when ground, it is actually slightly reddish pink. It has a sulfurous aroma and taste and across India is quite commonly used on salted nuts. There is really no substitution for this unique flavor. These spiced cashews make a wonderful addition to salads like Bright Fruit Salad (page 97).

**MAKES 8 SERVINGS**

2 tablespoons canola oil

1 teaspoon cayenne powder

1/2 teaspoon fresh finely ground black pepper

1/4 teaspoon black salt

1/2 teaspoon kosher salt

1 pound raw cashews

In a large skillet over low heat, warm the oil. Add the cayenne powder, black pepper, black salt, and kosher salt. Cook and stir for 1 minute; the spices should be very aromatic. Add the cashews, turning and coating them well with the spiced oil. Continue to cook, stirring constantly, until the cashews are blistered and a mottled brown, about 4 minutes.

There are three kinds of black salt, each used for different purposes; therefore be sure you buy the correct type. Black ritual salt, or witch's salt, is not for consumption; it is used most often in incense. *Black lava salt* is sea salt filtered through charcoal, usually originating in Hawaii or Cyprus and used primarily as a finishing salt. Indian or Himalayan black salt is a volcanic salt that starts out as pink salt, but it is heated at extremely high temperatures, turning it a deep purple. When heated, residual trace impurities of sulfites and sulfides are left behind, giving this salt a unique flavor similar to hard-boiled egg yolks. It is well worth the effort to track some down for your pantry.

teaspoon baking pow[der]
1½ cups milk
1 tablespoon salt
vanilla extract
2 large eggs, separated, plus 2
egg whites
1 stick melted salted butter
plus butter for serving

Preheat waffle iron to
regular setting.
Sift together the flou[r]
baking powder and salt
In a separate bowl, whis[k]
vanilla and 2 egg yolks together.

For the Cran[berry]
1 pound f[resh]
1 cup f[resh]
1 cup [sugar]

# serrano boiled peanuts

WHEN IT COMES TO BOILED PEANUTS, it doesn't matter which of my two Souths I look to for recipes because in either place they are consumed with passionate zeal. The only difference lies in the name: in India, peanuts are called groundnuts. This legume is an essential crop in India and is grown extensively as an oil crop. But, like in the US, peanuts are boiled, roasted, ground, and stir-fried. Any raw peanut is good for boiling. Not all peanuts sold in grocery stores are distinguished by variety. Many boiled peanut connoisseurs, however, seek out the Valencia variety for its sweet taste and the Virginia variety for its large kernel size.

Nothing beats a peanut for easy access to protein, iron, and energy. Whether you are watching football, baseball, international soccer, or cricket on the television, these lip-searing boiled peanuts served with a cool beverage are game-day fan favorites.

**MAKES 8 SERVINGS**

1 pound fresh raw peanuts in shell

1/3 cup kosher salt

1 teaspoon turmeric

4 serrano chiles, split, with seeds

Rinse the peanuts several times. Combine the peanuts, 1 gallon water, salt, turmeric, and chiles in a 2-gallon stockpot and cover with a lid. Bring the peanuts to a boil over medium heat. Simmer the peanuts for 1½ hours or until tender. If needed, cook, covered for an additional 15 minutes, adding water to cover, if needed.

# fresh fruit *with* custard sauce

IN INDIA THE ONE SWEET FOUND AT EVERY INDIAN RESTAURANT featuring a tea time is fruit salad with custard. This holds true in five-star hotels all the way down to simple neighborhood cafés. Families who gather around the home tea table regularly enjoy their own version of fruit and custard. India has a rich heritage of highlighting its abundance of fruits at the end of meals. This fruit salad recipe can be made with any combination of ripe seasonal fruits. In my case, if it were possible, I would insist on mangoes all year-round, but alas, the finest fresh mangoes only appear for three to four months of the year. Ripe purple plums are an excellent substitution if mangoes aren't peaking.

**MAKES 4 SERVINGS**

1<sup>1</sup>/2 cups whole milk

<sup>2</sup>/3 cup white granulated sugar

6 large egg yolks

1/2 teaspoon pure vanilla extract

1 cup fresh mango cubes

1 cup seedless green grapes, sliced in halves

1/2 cup fresh blueberries

1 cup fresh strawberries, hulled and quartered

In a medium saucepan over medium heat, add the milk and sugar; whisk the milk constantly for 4 minutes.

In a medium bowl, whisk together the egg yolks and slowly incorporate the hot milk into the egg mixture, whisking constantly for about a minute. Over a low heat, return the mixture back to the saucepan, whisking constantly for 5 minutes or until slightly thickened. (The custard should be thick enough to coat the back of a spoon; you want to keep the flame low and not let the mixture come to a simmer or the eggs will curdle.)

Remove from heat and add the vanilla. Immediately, strain the custard into a small bowl. Place in refrigerator to cool with a piece of plastic wrap pressed to the surface to prevent a skin from forming on top.

Serve the cooled custard over the fruit.

**NOTES:** *Don't wander off while making the custard sauce. The sauce will scorch easily. Be sure to use a heavy-bottomed saucepan and a flame tamer if the stove burner flame seems too high.*

# rice sopping bread

THESE YEASTED, PUFFY, STEAMED, COCONUT-LACED RICE CAKE ROUNDS are sliced and served much like American southerners serve cornbread. Delicious practically any time of day or night.

1½ cups jasmine rice

1½ cups grated fresh coconut

1 cup cooked jasmine rice

½ teaspoon active dry yeast

3 tablespoons white granulated sugar

½ teaspoon kosher salt

Coconut oil, to grease the pans

Soak the rice for 2 hours in 2 cups of water; strain the rice and set aside.

In a blender, add the soaked rice, grated coconut, cooked rice, yeast, sugar, and salt; pour just enough water to cover the ingredients in the blender, about 2 cups of water (make sure you don't add too much water). Blend to a smooth consistency, a little thicker than pancake batter. Pour this mixture into a large glass bowl, cover with plastic wrap, and set the dough aside for 2 hours. The dough will rise.

Grease two 8-inch cake pans. Mix the dough with a wooden spatula and pour the batter into two equal portions into the pans. (The pans should be three-quarters full.)

Place the pans in a steamer basket set over boiling water; cover and steam for 20 minutes. Remove the cakes from the steamer and cut each rice cake into six slices. Serve warm.

# banana beignets

I GUESS WHEN PEOPLE THINK BEIGNETS, THEY THINK NEW ORLEANS. Well, I grew up eating something very similar in Kerala: my mother would take overripe bananas and make these delicious treats at tea time. My addition is a big pinch of finely ground white pepper dusted along with the confectioners' sugar and nutmeg over the top. Quick, simple, and delicious alongside a warm cup of chai.

MAKES 25 TO 30 BEIGNETS

1/3 cup white granulated sugar

1 large egg

1 cup overripe bananas, mashed

2 cups cake flour

1/2 cup whole milk

2 teaspoons baking powder

1/2 teaspoon kosher salt

1 1/2 teaspoons freshly grated nutmeg, divided

2 tablespoons confectioners' sugar

1/2 teaspoon white pepper, finely ground

2 cups canola oil

In a large bowl, whisk together the sugar and egg. Add the bananas, flour, milk, baking powder, salt, and 1 teaspoon of the nutmeg to the egg mixture. Whisk until the batter is smooth.

In a small sifter, combine the remaining 1/2 teaspoon of nutmeg, the confectioners' sugar, and white pepper.

Heat 2 cups of oil in a deep, heavy skillet to 375°F. Line a tray with paper towels and set aside until time to drain the beignets.

Drop tablespoons of the batter into the hot oil and cook for about 20 seconds on each side, or until puffy and golden on all sides. Remove the beignets from the oil, letting the excess oil drip back in the skillet, then further drain on the tray lined with paper towels. Dust the beignets with the spiced confectioners' sugar. Grate additional nutmeg over the doughnuts, if desired. Serve at once.

# dutch cake rusk

RUSK IS A TYPE OF BREAD, QUITE SIMILAR TO BISCOTTI, made from scratch and twice baked. When it first comes out of the oven, rusk is very much like cake, but it is sliced, allowed to cool, then popped back in to dry and crisp at a lower temperature. The finished slices have a crunchy texture, much like that of Melba toast, and stay crisp in a tin for weeks, a quality much appreciated by sailors. A favored bread for long voyages, it also soothes the gums of teething babies.

Historically, coastal India was tremendously important to the global Dutch and Portuguese spice trade, so finding rusk as a common tea-time holdover is not surprising. Rusk did not originate in the Netherlands or Belgium. Nearly every region of the globe has its own version. The Dutch called it *beshcuit,* but it was the same as rusk or, in Hindi, *khasta.* Actually, the origin of the word *rusk* is probably Spanish, or maybe Portuguese. So what makes this recipe Dutch? Heck if I know. My family never used any other name for it!

Regular customers at Spice to Table have taken to spending an afternoon dipping these crunchy vanilla cake slices in my signature chai (page 118). It makes for a nice afternoon ritual and a great way to regroup and wrap up a day's work.

8 tablespoons (1 stick) unsalted butter, at room temperature

1 teaspoon pure vanilla extract

3/4 cup superfine white granulated sugar (see notes)

3 large eggs, at room temperature

1 cup unbleached all-purpose flour

1 teaspoon baking powder

1/2 teaspoon kosher salt

Heat the oven to 325°F. Grease an 8 x 8-inch baking pan.

Using an electric mixer, whip the butter for 3 minutes, or until very creamy. Add the vanilla extract and gradually whip in the sugar. Whip the mixture for 3 minutes, or until fluffy. Add the eggs one at a time and whip for 3 minutes. Gradually add the flour, baking powder, and salt. Whisk for 3 minutes, or until the batter is thick and well combined with no lumps, taking care to scrape the bottom and side of the bowl well.

Pour the batter into the baking pan. Bake for 40 minutes, or until a toothpick comes out clean. Place the cake in the pan on a cooling rack to cool for 10 minutes. Lower the oven temperature to 300°F.

Slice the cake into twelve half-inch-wide pieces, then slice each one down the center to form twenty-four pieces. Gently move the slices to a baking sheet with 1 inch spacing between each. Return the slices to the oven and bake 10 minutes. Flip the cake slices over and bake until dry and crisp, about 10 minutes. Remove slices from baking sheet and cool on a cooling rack.

**NOTES:** *Superfine sugar melts quicker and gives recipes a less grainy texture; always try to use it when specified. This is not to be confused with confectioners' sugar, which contains cornstarch to keep it from clumping. Most grocery stores stock it, but you can make superfine sugar at home by putting 1 cup plus two teaspoons of regular granulated sugar in a food processor and pulsing for 30 seconds to yield 1 cup of superfine sugar.*

# sultana semolina cashew sheera

FOOD SERVED IN HINDU TEMPLES IN INDIA IS CONSIDERED SACRED and known as *prasad*. Rich or poor, no matter your station in life, when you walk into a temple in India, there will be food for you to eat. *Sheera*, a sweet and simple semolina treat, is often placed in a bowl made out of lotus leaves and handed by the priest to devotees upon arrival and during ceremonies.

I may hail from a region of India that was predominantly Christian, but the majority of the people in India follow Hinduism. I enjoyed every festival from Diwali, the festival of lights, to Holi, the festival of colors. These holidays may not have been celebrated in my home, but they were celebrated in many of our friends' homes. We invited non-Christian friends into our home on holidays like Christmas and Easter, and I was, likewise, a guest in their homes on their religious holidays. Food is central for all religious celebrations in India, whether in everyday homes or in the temples and churches.

**MAKES 6 SERVINGS**

½ cup ghee

1 cup semolina flour

1½ cups whole milk, at room temperature

1½ cups water, at room temperature

1 cup white granulated sugar

2 tablespoons sultanas or golden raisins

18 to 20 roasted cashews

1 teaspoon green cardamom powder

In a medium nonstick skillet, heat the ghee over a low flame; add the semolina and stir for 6 minutes, or until the semolina is golden brown (you have to keep stirring so the semolina does not burn).

Add the room-temperature milk and water; mix well and cook for 2 minutes, while stirring continuously.

Add the sugar, raisins, cashews, and cardamom powder; mix well. Cover and cook on low for 6 minutes, stirring occasionally, until the sheera is the consistency of very thick cooked grits.

Serve immediately or at room temperature.

CHAPTER FOUR

# dinner &
# accompaniments

*If I'm not teaching a class or hosting a dinner at Third Space, my evenings are pretty laid back.*

◆—◆—◆—◆—◆—◆—◆—◆—◆—◆—◆—◆

Whether lounging at home with Ethan or helping him with homework, there is always a pot of chai brewing on my stove top. More often than not when my neighbor Alice pops in to say hello, Ethan and his friends gather in our yard for an impromptu game, or friends drop by for a visit, staying for dinner, or a cookout rounds out our day.

Other days may find my staff and me cooking dishes for hundreds of guests at charity fundraisers or preparing recipes in bulk for events at my son's school. On these days, dinner for me means grabbing a late-night bite from the fridge after the lights are out and both boy and dog are tucked in for the night. Like many mothers who juggle work and home, I find I have become quite adept at turning leftovers into centerpiece dishes—something that I am thankful for having learned from my own busy mother.

A large part of this chapter showcases dishes from the sea. The smell and sound of the sea along with the good people raised and living on its shores influenced my early years in Kerala. Seafood was the first food I chose for joining my two Souths. This chapter also includes an array of main dishes, side dishes, and accompanying condiments for virtually every sort of dinner. It won't matter if you are cooking for a speedy weeknight, a slow Sunday, or a big dinner party or making a dish ahead for a potluck; there's a recipe here for every situation.

# duck egg curry *or* duck mutta roast

I MET BOBBY PALAYAM, Ethan's dad, at a New Year's Eve party on Long Island, New York, in 1998. Our love of food and all things Keralan was a strong common bond. I learned early on that Bobby loves eggs in any form or shape, for breakfast, lunch, or dinner or anytime in between. Boiled egg curry or, as it's called in Kerala, *mutta roast* was cooked often in our home. This dish can be found at roadside stalls late at night along highways in southern India. Similar to the American belief that good food can be found at truck stops, truck drivers in India claim the best food is served up after midnight at these highway pit stops. The following rather simple dish made with caramelized onions in a tomato base served with boiled duck eggs is a dish that will definitely charm an egg lover. You can always use extra-large or jumbo chicken eggs if you can't find duck eggs, though the large yolks of duck eggs add much to the dish. This egg curry is great served alongside Coconut Milk Rice (page 195) with Rice Sopping Bread (page 145) for lapping up every speck of the flavorful sauce.

8 large duck eggs

4 tablespoons coconut oil

2 large red onions, thinly sliced

1 tablespoon peeled, chopped fresh ginger

4 fresh or dry bay leaves

4 Thai chiles, slit in half lengthwise (leave the seeds in)

4 large Roma tomatoes, sliced

1 tablespoon sweet paprika

1/2 teaspoon tumeric

1 teaspoon salt

**MAKES 4 SERVINGS**

Place the duck eggs in a 2-quart pot, cover with cold water, and bring to a boil over high heat. Once the water is boiling, immediately remove the pot from the heat and let stand, covered, for 12 minutes. Crack the eggs just slightly and cool under running water. Remove the shells and cut each egg in half lengthwise and set aside.

In a heavy-bottomed pan over medium heat, add the coconut oil. Add the onions and cook for 8 minutes, or until the onions are golden brown. Add the ginger and bay leaves and cook for 1 minute, stirring constantly. Add the chiles and tomatoes and cook, stirring every so often, for another 8 minutes, or until the tomatoes cook down and the oil starts separating from the mixture. Add the paprika, turmeric, and salt and cook for another 2 minutes, stirring often. Add the boiled duck eggs to the masala mixture, egg yolk facing up. Spoon masala over all the eggs; cook another 2 minutes. Remove from heat and serve.

# green cardamom shrimp étouffée

IN QUILON, A PORT CITY near where I grew up, the flavors, spices, and cooking styles have been blending in a cross-cultural melting pot for centuries. The Gulf Coast port city of New Orleans owes its culinary traditions to such a melting pot of influences as well. Both cities were my inspiration for this dish, which continues the idea of culinary assimilation; it's my reimagining of the classic Creole dish, spotlighting the green cardamom so often found in dishes along my native shore.

**MAKES 6 SERVINGS**

4 tablespoons (½ stick) unsalted butter

¼ cup unbleached all-purpose flour

2 medium onions, peeled and chopped

2 large green bell peppers, seeded and chopped

6 medium celery stalks and leaves, chopped

3 garlic cloves, finely chopped

1 large tomato, diced or 1 cup drained, canned, diced tomatoes

2 teaspoons fresh coarsely ground black peppercorns, divided

2 teaspoons green cardamom powder, divided

2 teaspoons ginger powder, divided

2 teaspoons coriander powder, divided

1 teaspoon kosher salt, divided

2 pounds medium shrimp (21 to 25 count per pound), peeled and deveined, reserving shells for stock

3 cups shrimp stock

2 cups cooked basmati white rice

In a large Dutch oven over medium heat, melt the butter. Add the flour and cook, stirring continuously for 6 to 8 minutes to make a smooth golden roux, making sure to break up any lumps. Add the onions, bell peppers, celery, and garlic to the roux and mix well. Continue cooking and stirring for 3 minutes, or until the vegetables are tender.

Add the tomatoes and shrimp stock to the pot, and then add 1 teaspoon each of the black pepper, ginger, cardamom, and coriander and ½ teaspoon of the salt.

Bring the sauce to a boil, and then reduce to a simmer over medium-low heat.

Season the shrimp with the remaining black pepper, ginger, coriander, cardamom, and salt. Add the shrimp to the pot and stir. Cook the shrimp until they are cooked through, about 4 to 5 minutes. Serve the shrimp and sauce over the cooked white rice.

**NOTE:** *In a pinch, you can substitute clam juice for the shrimp stock in this recipe.*

# mussels *in* light broth

*RASAM* AS PREPARED IN MOST HOMES IN SOUTHERN INDIA uses either tamarind or tomatoes as the base. It is a piquant broth poured over steaming hot rice. In our home both in Kerala and America, *rasam* was a staple part of everyday meals. One night when I was a teenager, I was out to dinner with my brother Tom in New York City's Little Italy and ate mussels cooked in a light tomato broth very reminiscent of *rasam*. I couldn't wait to get home, buy fresh mussels, and cook them in *rasam*. This dish has made its rounds in my kitchens for close to three decades now. Make sure to have some fresh crusty bread to soak up the tomato mussel broth.

**MAKES 4 SERVINGS**

2 tablespoons canola oil

1 tablespoon peeled, finely chopped fresh ginger

2 garlic cloves, finely chopped

1 tablespoon cumin seeds (coarsely crushed in a mortar and pestle)

10 to 12 whole black peppercorns, coarsely crushed in a mortar and pestle

1/4 teaspoon asafoetida powder

1 teaspoon kosher salt

16 ounces canned crushed tomatoes or 2 cups peeled, diced fresh tomatoes

1/2 cup finely chopped cilantro leaves and stems

2 pounds fresh mussels

1 tablespoon tempered oil

In a 4-quart pot over medium heat, add the oil. Add the ginger, garlic, cumin, black peppercorns, asafoetida, and salt. Cook, stirring constantly, for 1 minute. Add the tomatoes and cilantro and cook for 5 minutes, stirring occasionally. Add 2 cups of water and cook for 8 minutes on a low heat. Add the mussels, cover and cook for 5 to 6 minutes, or until the mussels are opened. Remove from the heat. Transfer the mussels and broth to a serving bowl and finish with the tempered oil.

**NOTES**: *Mussels attach themselves to stable surfaces using thin, sticky, weedy membranes referred to as "beards," which must be removed before cooking. Most farm-raised mussels purchased in grocery stores have already been debearded. If the beard is still attached, grasp it with your fingers and pull it downward toward the hinged end of the shell. Pull firmly until it comes out and discard it. Place mussels in a colander in the sink, and run cold water over them to get rid of any visible dirt or grit on the outer shells. Using a vegetable brush, scrub each shell under running water. Overlooked grit can ruin a dish.*

## TEMPERED OIL

2 tablespoons oil

10 to 12 curry leaves

1 teaspoon brown mustard seeds

In a small pan over medium heat, add oil. Add the curry leaves and mustard seeds; when the mustard seeds begin to pop, remove the oil from the flame, about 30 seconds. Drizzle the oil over the mussels and broth.

# shishito pepper crawfish
## *with* polenta

I AM NOT ONE TO BE STARSTRUCK, but before James Beard Award–winning chef Anne Quatrano and I became friends, I was starry eyed every time I saw Anne. She is to me the epitome of everything I aspire to be in the culinary world. She is a visionary and inspires me with her thoughtful work.

Here's the sweet story of how Anne and I had one of our first very personal encounters. I was cooking at Cardamom Hill one morning, and for some reason I couldn't stop thinking of Anne, so I packed an earthen pot with a *biryani* I had made, attached a note that read "I hope you enjoy this for lunch today!" and had a waiter deliver it to Star Provisions, one of Anne's businesses. That evening around five thirty, right before service at Cardamom Hill, the receptionist came into the kitchen and said "Anne Quatrano is here to see you"; my knees buckled and I ran out to receive her. She stood there with the earthen pot and a big smile on her beautiful face. She said, "My mama taught me never to return an empty pot, so I made you dinner." She had made me polenta with fried shishito peppers and shrimp. We have been friends ever since that day. And I am still, as always, in awe of her generosity, her sisterhood, and her love. I can truly say I love Anne!

I know you will love sharing this peppery crawfish version with friends or use it to fill a borrowed pot before returning it.

## POLENTA

3 tablespoons ghee

2 medium Vidalia or sweet yellow onions, finely chopped (about 1½ cups)

4 garlic cloves, finely chopped

6 sage leaves, cut into very thin strips

6 cups low-sodium chicken stock

1½ teaspoons kosher salt

1¾ cups yellow cornmeal

In a heavy-bottomed pot over medium heat, add the ghee and the onions and cook for 3 minutes until the onions are translucent. Add the garlic and sage and cook for another 30 seconds. Add the chicken stock and bring stock to a boil. Add the salt. Gradually whisk in the cornmeal. Reduce the heat to low and cook until the mixture thickens and the cornmeal is tender, stirring often, about 15 minutes.

## CRAWFISH

3 tablespoons canola oil

2 medium Vidalia or yellow sweet onions, thinly sliced

½ pound shishito peppers, whole, stems on

1 teaspoon fresh coarsely ground black peppercorns

1 teaspoon garlic powder

1 teaspoon turmeric powder

1 teaspoon kosher salt

2 pounds crawfish, steamed and shelled, or frozen crawfish tails with fat, thawed

1 cup coconut milk

In a large skillet over high heat, add the oil and the onions and cook until golden brown, about 6 minutes. Add the shishito peppers and cook on high flame for 3 minutes until the pepper skins blister; add the pepper, garlic powder, turmeric, and salt and stir for 1 minute. Add the crawfish tail meat and continue cooking on a high flame until the crawfish have a nice sear on them, about 3 minutes. Add the coconut milk, bring to a quick simmer, and remove from flame.

Serve the polenta in a bowl and spoon the crawfish and peppers over the polenta.

# friday fish dinner

AS I PREVIOUSLY MENTIONED, I AM A MEMBER OF A FIVE-GENERATION Roman Catholic family (we are waiting with open minds to see how our newest generation's faith will be expressed). Although not exactly common in India, there are a significant number of Catholics in India, particularly on the Southern Peninsula, where practitioners likely trace their family conversions back to the early 1500s, when long-distance Portuguese mariners and missionaries arrived on the Malabar Coast. So, like many Catholics households, on Fridays we avoided eating the meat of any warm-blooded animal. Living in a country where some people refrain from eating garlic or onions for fear of killing small creatures (Jains), where cows roam freely and are honored as sacred (Hindus), and where certain foods are prohibited unless slaughtered in a precise manner according to religious standards (Muslims), abstaining from eating meat seemed par for the course to our family. All around the world, people practice their faith with food—expressed either via prohibition or celebration. In America, many foods are also closely associated with religious ritual, although many people do not even realize it. But whether it's for reasons of faith or reasons of taste, nothing quite beats a Friday fish dinner.

My version is a king mackerel curry with the delicious draw of *kodampuli*—a dried, smoked fruit that delivers a distinct sour flavor to many seafood and curry recipes. That flavor along with the heat of green chiles, ginger powder, and Kashmiri chili powder and a hint of the burnt-sugar flavor of fenugreek all serve to introduce a full-on Keralan weekend. Finished with oil tempered with curry leaves and the pungent pluck of black mustard seeds, this may very well become a kick-off-the-weekend Friday favorite in your household, too.

4 pieces kodampuli

3 king mackerel steaks (about 2 pounds), each steak cut into 3 to 4 pieces

1 large Roma tomato, quartered

2 small Thai green chiles

3 garlic cloves, finely chopped

2 teaspoons peeled, chopped fresh ginger

1/2 teaspoon fenugreek powder

2 teaspoons Kashmiri chili powder

1 teaspoon turmeric powder

3 tablespoons coconut oil, divided

1/4 teaspoon fenugreek seeds

2 shallots, peeled and thinly sliced

15 curry leaves, divided

1 1/4 teaspoons kosher salt

1 teaspoon black mustard seeds

3 whole dried red chiles

In a large bowl, soak the *kodampuli* in 1 cup warm water for 10 minutes. Add the fish pieces and marinate in the *kodampuli*-infused water for 15 minutes or up to 30 minutes.

Meanwhile, in a blender or food processor, combine 1/2 cup water, tomato, green chiles, garlic, ginger, fenugreek powder, chili powder, and turmeric and blend to make a smooth paste.

In a large, deep skillet, heat 2 tablespoons of the coconut oil over medium heat until hot. Add the 1/4 teaspoon of fenugreek seeds and cook briefly until the seeds start to crackle, about 15 seconds. Add the shallots and 5 of the curry leaves. Cook and stir until the shallots are tender, about 4 minutes. Add the blended spice paste and stir to combine, add salt. Add the fish along with the water to the shallots. Increase the heat to high and gently stir to coat the fish with the sauce as the mixture comes to a boil. Reduce the heat to low and simmer, gently swirling and shaking the skillet occasionally to mix the sauce and taking care not to break the fish pieces, until the fish is cooked through and the sauce has thickened, about 10 minutes. Remove from heat. Remove the *kodampuli*.

In a small saucepan, heat the remaining coconut oil until hot. Add the mustard seeds, 10 curry leaves, and dried red chiles; cook and stir for 1 minute. Gently fold the flavored oil and toasted spices into the fish curry. Serve warm over rice.

# banana leaf grilled catfish *with* watermelon rind chow chow

1 teaspoon turmeric powder

1 teaspoon Kashmiri chili powder

2 teaspoons garlic powder

1/2 teaspoon kosher salt

Juice of 3 limes (about 1/3 cup)

2 tablespoons canola oil

6 catfish fillets (6 ounces)

Six banana leaves, fresh or frozen, thawed

Mix the turmeric, chili powder, garlic powder, salt, lime juice, 1 table-spoon of water, and oil to form a paste.

Pat the fillets dry with paper towels and apply the spice paste generously on both sides; set aside and marinate for 30 minutes or overnight.

While the fish is marinating, roast the banana leaves on an open flame. (Run the leaves over an open flame for about 5 seconds on each side; you will see the essential oils of the leaf come through. This process makes the banana leaf pliable and easy to work with and brings out the flavor.) Cut the banana leaves into 10 x 4-inch strips. Place a fish fillet in the center of each strip and fold either side into the center; place each wrapped fillet seam-side down.

Get the grill ready. Heat a gas grill to medium high or prepare medium ash-covered coals.

Place the banana leaf packets seam-side down on the grill, 6 to 8 inches above the medium coals, and grill for 5 minutes. Flip the parcels and grill for another 5 minutes on the other side.

Serve the banana-leaf-wrapped fillets with Watermelon Rind Chow Chow.

# WATERMELON RIND CHOW CHOW

MY TWO SOUTHS HAVE YET another culinary cousin, with virtually only the name being the differing factor. I'm referring to the "chutney versus chow chow" debate. In India, chutney is a side dish that can vary from a pickled tomato relish to a ground peanut condiment to a yogurt cucumber mint dip. In the southern states, chow chow mainly refers to a relish made from pickled vegetables ranging from green tomatoes, cabbage, chayote, red tomatoes, and onions to carrots, asparagus, beans, cauliflower, and peas. Actually, about the only real difference between chutney and chow chow is that chutney is more spreadable than the chunkier chow chow. In both incarnations, ingredients vary as do the savory or sweet. It really boils down to personal preferences as to what goes in it and what you call it. Try mango or peaches in place of the watermelon rind in this recipe. I also love this chunky relish with baked ham or Mint Masala Roasted Chicken (page 174).

4 tablespoons vegetable oil

4 whole star anise

1 teaspoon brown mustard seeds

1 teaspoon cumin seeds

1 teaspoon paprika

1 teaspoon kosher salt

2 tablespoons white granulated sugar

2 cups finely diced watermelon rind (white part only)

**MAKES 1 PINT, 6 SERVINGS**

In a large skillet over medium-high heat, heat the oil. Add the star anise, mustard seeds, cumin seeds, paprika, salt, and sugar. Cook, stirring, for about 1 minute. Add the watermelon rind and cook and stir for 5 minutes, or until the rind is tender. Allow to cool, then place in a glass jar and store in the refrigerate for up to a week. You can also process for canning for longer storage, or it can be frozen in a plastic freezer bag for up to three months.

# coconut oil poached snapper

WHEN I FIRST MOVED TO ATLANTA and long before I realized where my cooking life would lead me, I lived close to Star Provisions, a culinary dream stop featuring individual markets for gourmet ingredients, food-related shopping, and incredible prepared meals. Star Provisions was often a three-times-a-week stop for me to buy stunningly fresh seafood to cook at home. I became friends with the dear folks behind the butcher blocks and food counters. On a particular visit, one of the chefs challenged me to a "secret ingredient cook-off" with snapper as our foil for battle. Even with such stiff competition, I feel I triumphed with this recipe that features Meyer lemon, fresh thyme, and delicate, moist fillets of snapper. The coconut oil imbues a magically lush texture to the fillets in this simple preparation. Halibut, catfish, and cod are also delicious prepared in this method.

**MAKES 4 SERVINGS**

½ cup coconut oil

1½ cups low-sodium vegetable stock plus 1 tablespoon stock

2 Meyer lemons, zested and juiced plus 4 Meyer lemon wedges for garnish (see notes)

1 teaspoon kosher salt

2 sprigs fresh thyme plus additional sprigs for garnish

4 red snapper fillets (about 2 pounds), skin on

1 tablespoon cornstarch

In a 10-inch skillet or one large enough for two fish fillets to lie flat, combine the coconut oil, 1½ cups vegetable stock, lemon juice and zest, salt, and thyme and bring to a simmer over low heat, about 5 minutes.

Add two of the snapper fillets skin-side down and poach the fish on the lowest heat setting for 10 minutes. Gently remove each fillet with a slotted spatula to a platter and tent with foil. Repeat with the two remaining fish fillets.

Increase the heat to high and cook, stirring occasionally, until the poaching liquid is reduced by half, about 5 minutes. Remove any woody thyme stems from the liquid.

In a small cup, mix 1 tablespoon vegetable stock with the cornstarch until smooth. Whisk in the cornstarch slurry and bring to a boil for 1 minute or until the sauce is slightly thickened. Pour the sauce over the fish, and garnish with the lemon wedges and fresh thyme sprigs; serve warm.

**NOTES:** *Meyer lemons are named for Frank N. Meyer, an early twentieth-century fruit importer who collected a sample of the variety on a trip to China. Their taste is like a cross between a lemon and a mandarin orange; they are sweeter and less acidic than regular lemons. The fruit is in season from November to April. If Meyer lemons are unavailable, substitute one tangerine and one lemon in this recipe.*

# prawn pan roast *or* chemmen

EVERY TIME I SEE PRAWNS in the market, I flash to a vision of my younger self, back home in Kerala, running down the sandy walkway to catch up with my mother as she opened our orange, insignia-laden Carmel Compound gate to meet fishermen's wives dressed in vibrant saris. The women would walk from household to household along the azure coastline with coconut husk baskets filled with fresh prawns perched skillfully on their heads. I would cling to my mother's legs as she inspected the day's catch, listening in as she and the women swapped news, as she selected only the best prawns for purchase. I hope that my own son is making mental movies as he helps me select our purchases and we visit with farmers and fishermen, and that in years to come he will realize his memories are the culmination of the heritage of our two Souths.

These prawns are buffed up with a masala featuring flavor-enhancing dried shrimp and chopped fresh ginger, then bathed in coconut milk infused with bay and sweet shallots.

¼ cup dried shrimp (see notes)

2 tablespoons peeled, finely chopped fresh ginger

¼ cup coconut milk

2 tablespoons coconut oil

2 medium shallots, peeled and thinly sliced

2 fresh bay leaves

1 tablespoon hot paprika

1 teaspoon turmeric powder

1 tablespoon tomato paste

1 teaspoon kosher salt

2 pounds freshwater prawns or jumbo shrimp (20 to 30 count), peeled and deveined

**MAKES 6 SERVINGS**

In a blender or food processor, combine the dried shrimp, ginger, and coconut milk. Blend to make a thick paste; set aside.

In a large skillet over medium heat, heat the coconut oil until hot. Add the shallots and bay leaves. Cook, stirring occasionally, until the shallots are golden, about 6 minutes. Add the paprika and turmeric and cook, stirring, for 1 minute. Add the tomato paste, shrimp paste mixture, salt, and ¼ cup of water; stir well.

Cook the mixture over medium heat until the prawns are cooked through and turn pink, about 5 minutes, taking care to avoid overcooking the shrimp, as they will continue to cook after being removed from the heat. Remove the skillet from the heat. Allow to sit uncovered for carryover heat to cook the shrimp through, about 10 minutes. Remove the bay leaves and serve.

**NOTES:** *Dried shrimp are a flavor powerhouse. Often found in Asian and Latin American dishes, the tiny, sundried shellfish lend a salty flavor, much like anchovy paste or fish sauce. The smell is much more potent than the flavor once it is incorporated in the sauce. When shopping, look for whole dried shrimp with a nice coral color; gray or a washed-out pink color can mean the shrimp are old and stale or of poor quality to begin with. These briny secret agents of flavor add much depth to this dish.*

## PRAWN OR SHRIMP?

There is a lot of confusion regarding the differences, for sure. The word *shrimp* was not part of my vocabulary until I arrived in the United States; the sweet crustaceans from the sea by my home were always referred to as prawns. There is a difference: prawns are larger, with larger legs that include claws on three pairs, and they have what is known as branching gills. Shrimp, on the other hand, are generally smaller with claws on only two pairs of legs, and their gills are laminar, or plate-like. To complicate things further, in the US you may also find similar creatures sold as langoustine or Italian scampi prawns; belonging to the crab family, these are neither shrimp nor lobster. They grow 9 to 10 inches long but have much smaller claws than lobsters, making their tail meat the star. Then there are freshwater prawns, which look a bit like a cross between a lobster and a shrimp with a superlong second set of legs, but they actually belong to their very own genus. The bottom line? For this recipe—and most others requiring the larger creatures—any prawn, shrimp, langoustine, or freshwater prawn that is sold with a count of fifteen or fewer to a pound is fine. Whichever you use, be sure not to overcook, as the bigger crustaceans tend to get quite rubbery and stringy when not cooked to perfection. Also, don't forget to use the heads, tails, and shells for stock (page 101).

One final comment on prawns: Lauren Farms in Leland, Mississippi, ships sweet freshwater prawns all over the world. If you find yourself in the Delta, stop by and visit this wonderful mom-and-pop operation run by Steve and Dolores Fratesi. Plan a field trip to the Fratesis' annual bankside sale in the late fall, and stock the freezer with their lapis-lazuli-shelled beauties.

# marcus's turkey kheema sloppy joes

MY NEPHEW MARCUS IS VERY DEAR TO ME. I refer to him as my firstborn. He has brought nothing but joy to my life. He has exceeded all expectations and excelled academically in ways we never knew were possible. As a well-rounded young man, he enjoys playing his ukulele and acoustic guitar and listening to heavy metal as much as he loves doing cardiovascular stem cell research. Ethan has not had to look too far afield for a role model; Marcus has been a fine big brother to my young son. Did I mention Marcus loves to eat? He loves for me to cook for him and devours pretty much anything put before him. A good turkey *kheema*, the Indian version of a sloppy joe, is one of his favorites. A soft bun with this saucy filling piled inside and a side of Roasted Garlicky Potato Salad (page 201) keeps him fueled for his studies.

**MAKES 4 SERVINGS**

1 tablespoon coconut oil

1 large yellow onion, chopped (about 1 cup)

1 small red bell pepper, seeded and chopped (about 1/2 cup)

1 1/4 pounds ground turkey

1 tablespoon packed dark-brown sugar

2 teaspoons fresh coarsely ground black peppercorns

2 teaspoons garam masala

2 teaspoons garlic powder

1 teaspoon kosher salt

1 tablespoon Worcestershire sauce

1 cup tomato sauce

4 large sesame seed hamburger buns, buttered and toasted

Heat a large skillet over medium-high heat and add the oil. Add the onions and peppers to the pan and cook until the onions are translucent, about 3 minutes. Add the ground turkey and spread the meat around the pan and begin to break it up; cook for 2 minutes. Add the brown sugar, black pepper, garam masala, garlic powder, and salt; stir well for a minute. Keep cooking the turkey for 8 minutes, or until the meat has browned. Add the Worcestershire sauce to the turkey and cook for 2 minutes. Add the tomato sauce to the pan, stirring to combine. Reduce the heat to simmer and cook the mixture 5 minutes longer. Remove from the heat. Spoon the sloppy turkey onto toasted, buttered bun bottoms and cover with bun tops.

# fishwife's pie

*IT WAS A DARK AND STORMY NIGHT . . .* and I found myself at home facing what many busy parents dread: a hungry child and a virtually empty pantry! Not wanting to face a rainy drive to the market and resisting the urge to just order out pizza, like the fabled, bawdy fishwife of old, I uttered an oath under my breath and surveyed the kitchen and fridge. I discovered I did have fresh potatoes and carrots, along with green peas and some nice, thick catfish fillets in the freezer. And of course, I had my ever-ready *masal dhabba*—a stainless steel tin containing a collection of spices essential to any Indian kitchen—at hand. Looking over my ingredients, I came up with this savory take on shepherd's pie. It's seasoned with tried-and-true Old Bay Seasoning augmented with brown mustard seeds and topped with brown peaks of golden mashed potatoes. Since it contains fish rather than beef or lamb—and because of my oath under pressure—I decided to call it Fishwife's Pie.

6 medium small gold potatoes (2 pounds), peeled and quartered

2 teaspoons kosher salt

8 tablespoons (1 stick) unsalted butter, divided

2 teaspoons very finely chopped garlic

1 large yellow onion, peeled and finely chopped (about 1 cup)

½ teaspoon brown mustard seeds

1 teaspoon Old Bay Seasoning (see notes)

½ cup fresh or frozen green peas

2 medium carrots, peeled and diced (½ cup)

2 teaspoons fresh thyme leaves

5 to 7 catfish fillets or skinned boned catfish steaks (2 pounds), cut into 2-inch pieces

**MAKES ONE 10 X 8-INCH CASSEROLE, 6 SERVINGS**

Place the potatoes in a large pot, cover with 2 inches of water, and add the salt. Over high heat, boil the potatoes until tender, about 20 minutes. Drain off the water and mash the potatoes with 4 tablespoons of the butter and 2 teaspoons of the garlic. Set the mashed potatoes aside while preparing the fish filling.

In a large skillet over medium heat, melt the remaining 4 tablespoons of butter. Add the onion and cook, stirring frequently, until the onions are translucent and soft, about 5 minutes.

Add the mustard seeds and stir for 30 seconds. Add the Old Bay Seasoning, peas, carrots, and thyme and stir for 1 minute. Add the fish and cook, stirring occasionally for about 10 minutes, or until flaky and just cooked through.

Heat the oven to 400°F.

Place the fish along with all the sauce and vegetables in a 10 x 8-inch baking dish. Evenly distribute the mashed potatoes over the fish filling. Using a fork, rough up the surface of the potatoes to make lots of little peaks that will brown nicely when baking.

Bake the fish pie for 25 minutes, or until bubbly and the peaks are brown. If needed, broil for the last 3 minutes to brown the tops of the potatoes.

Remove the pie from the oven and let cool for 10 minutes before serving.

**NOTES:** *Old Bay Seasoning is the brand name of a blend of herbs and spices produced in Maryland by McCormick & Co. It is often used in crab recipes along the Atlantic coast. There is a lingering connection, bound and blended by spice, between my two Souths, and it is apparent in Old Bay Seasoning. It is kind of like a long-lost cousin of my beloved garam masala; the two blends share so many of the same ingredients. You can make a homemade version by combining the following:*

| | |
|---|---|
| 2 tablespoons bay leaf, crumbled | 1 teaspoon freshly grated nutmeg |
| 2 tablespoons celery salt | 1 teaspoon clove powder |
| 1 tablespoon dry mustard powder | 1 teaspoon allspice powder |
| 2 teaspoons finely ground black peppercorns | 1 teaspoon crushed red pepper flakes |
| 2 teaspoons ginger powder | 1/2 teaspoon mace powder |
| 2 teaspoons Kashmiri chili powder | 1/2 teaspoon green cardamom powder |
| 1 teaspoon finely ground white pepper | 1/4 teaspoon cinnamon powder |

Combine all ingredients and store in an airtight container. This seasoning blend will keep indefinitely.

# mint masala roasted chicken
## *with* fennel *and* potatoes

IF I HAD TO REQUEST A LAST MEAL, it would be this roasted bird. The whole process of seasoning a plump hen, tying it nice and tightly with butcher's twine, and then nestling it into a bed of colorful potatoes and fragrant fennel makes me feel so grounded, so . . . well, *at home*. Filling my house with the tantalizing aroma of mint and garlic with intriguing notes of fennel and citrus is always just wonderful. I truly enjoy making this dish as much as I love sharing it and devouring it.

1½ cups fresh spearmint leaves

3 serrano chiles, slit in half lengthwise

1 large garlic head, cut in half crosswise around the equator, plus 6 garlic cloves, peeled

Juice of 3 limes (6 tablespoons)

1½ teaspoons kosher salt

¼ cup olive oil

1 roasting chicken (5 to 6 pounds)

2 tablespoons unsalted butter, melted

1 lemon, halved

4 to 5 sprigs fresh thyme

1 large yellow onion, peeled, halved, and thickly sliced (about 1 cup)

1 large fennel bulb, cored and cut into wedges, reserving the top for garnish (see notes)

8 to 10 small potatoes, colored, new, or fingerlings (1 pound)

**MAKES 6 SERVINGS**

In a blender or food processor, blend the mint, serrano chiles, 6 garlic cloves, lime juice, salt, and ½ cup water to make a smooth paste. Spoon the paste into a small bowl and whisk in the olive oil.

Heat the oven to 425°F.

Remove the giblets from the chicken. Rinse the chicken inside and out and pat dry with paper towels. Using half of the mint paste and your fingers, season the chicken beneath the skin, inside the cavity, and all over the surface of the skin. Brush the chicken inside and out with the melted butter.

Stuff the chicken with the lemon, halved garlic bulb, and thyme. Tie the legs together with butcher's twine.

Scatter the onion, fennel, and potatoes in the bottom of a roasting pan and toss with the remaining mint paste. Place the chicken on top of the potatoes and tuck the wingtips under. Roast the chicken for 1½ hours, or until juices run clear and a thermometer reads 165°F when inserted in the thickest part of the thigh.

Remove the chicken and vegetables to a platter, spoon any pan drippings over the potatoes, and tent with foil to retain moisture. Let the chicken rest for 20 minutes to allow the juices to settle. Carve and serve with the roasted potatoes, onion, and fennel. Garnish with fennel fronds, if desired.

**NOTES:** *This recipe calls for a fennel bulb. While other parts of the plant are used as a spice, the bulb (or root) is a crisp vegetable that can be braised, grilled, sautéed, stewed, and even eaten raw. Fresh fennel is often found whole in markets with the bulb, stalks, and fronds intact. To cut fennel, simply lop off the stalks and fronds from the top of the bulb, retaining them for use as a spice or garnish or in stocks. (I put them in flower arrangements.) Cut the bulb in half, then cut out the woody bottom center section as you would a cabbage. Rather than imparting a licorice flavor, the fennel bulb imparts a slightly sweet, bright, spring-like quality to dishes.*

# weeknight fancy chicken *and* rice

IN INDIA, AS IN NORTH AMERICA, the origin of many chicken and rice recipes can be traced back to the influence of the Spanish and Portuguese explorers who brought along their recipes for *arroz con pollo*. Unfortunately, over the centuries, the original concoction of chicken and yellow rice mutated until the name "chicken and rice" now commonly refers to salty casseroles. We seldom see recipes using the delicate saffron that gives the rice its rich yellow color and nutty flavor, and many people protest that saffron is just too expensive for everyday cooking. Drawing on my experience with turmeric, I found a way to regain the integrity of this one-pot chicken and rice recipe, while keeping the convenience that makes it such a wonderful meal for hectic weeknights. The blend of green cardamom and star anise brings back the simple sophistication of the original chicken and rice standard. The garnish of glowing dried apricots, cilantro, and toasted almonds elevates the dish to elegance. And, finally, the bright yellow glow of turmeric returns the dish to its golden origins.

**MAKES 4 SERVINGS**

1/4 cup ghee

1 large yellow onion, peeled, halved and thinly sliced

6 green cardamom pods, crushed

3 star anise

1 1/4 teaspoons kosher salt, divided

6 garlic cloves, finely chopped

1 1/2 teaspoons turmeric powder

1 pound boneless, skinless chicken breasts, cut into 3/4-inch pieces

2 1/4 cups low-sodium chicken stock

1 1/2 cups basmati rice

1/4 cup chopped dried apricots

1/4 cup (2 ounces) sliced natural almonds, toasted

1/4 cup chopped cilantro leaves

In a 3-quart saucepan with a lid, melt the ghee over medium-high heat. Add the onion, cardamom, star anise, and 1/4 teaspoon of the salt. Cook, stirring frequently, until the onion is soft and a very deep golden brown, about 8 to 10 minutes. Add the garlic and turmeric; cook and stir for 2 minutes, or until very fragrant. Add the chicken and cook for 4 minutes, stirring to coat the chicken with the sauce.

Add the stock and remaining salt, increase the heat, and bring to a boil. Add the rice, stir, and cover. Reduce heat to low and simmer until the rice has absorbed the liquid, about 12 minutes. Remove from the heat and let stand, covered, for 12 minutes. Remove the lid and fluff the rice with a fork. Transfer the chicken and rice into a bowl, taking care to remove and discard the cardamom pods and star anise. Garnish with the apricots, almonds, and cilantro. Serve at once.

**NOTES:** *Try your favorite combination of dried fruits, nuts, and seeds as a garnish for this richly renewed chicken and rice one-pot dinner. Try dried cranberries, hazelnuts, or pine nuts as toppings for this lovely rice dish.*

# turmeric turkey potpie

ALTHOUGH WE DO HAVE VARIOUS HARVEST "THANKSGIVING" celebrations in India, I still consider Thanksgiving roast turkey as uniquely American fare. And even though I have delighted in adapting many American recipes over the years, I would not dare try to weigh in on the preparation of such a classic—not to mention finding myself in the middle of the whole "stuffing or dressing" debate! I will, however, make a recipe suggestion for the ever-enduring dilemma of leftover turkey. When it seems that the Thanksgiving bird will simply not stop giving, use this easy potpie as the final offering. It is so easy, you just may find yourself cooking turkey at other times of the year—just for the satisfaction of making and enjoying this lovely pastry-topped pie.

3 tablespoons unsalted butter

1 large yellow onion, peeled and diced (about 1 cup)

2 stalks celery, diced

1 teaspoon crushed red pepper flakes

1 teaspoon garam masala

1½ teaspoons garlic powder

½ teaspoon turmeric powder

1 teaspoon kosher salt

4 tablespoons unbleached all-purpose flour

3 cups turkey or chicken stock

1 cup heavy cream

2 medium carrots, peeled and diced (about 1 cup)

2 small gold potatoes, peeled and diced

3 cups boneless, cooked turkey, chopped

1 cup fresh or frozen green peas

1 tablespoon fresh thyme leaves

1 (14 x 9-inch) sheet frozen puff pastry (two 14-ounce packages), thawed

1 egg, beaten

In a 2-quart saucepan, melt the butter over medium heat. Add the onion and celery and cook, stirring frequently until tender, about 4 minutes. Stir in the red pepper flakes, garam masala, garlic powder, turmeric, salt, and flour. Stir until well blended, taking care to break up any lumps of flour. Gradually stir in the stock and heavy cream. Cook, stirring constantly for 8 minutes, or until thickened and bubbly.

Heat the oven to 350°F.

Stir the carrots and potatoes into the cream sauce. Reduce heat and simmer for 10 minutes, or until the carrots are just tender. Add the turkey, peas, and thyme and simmer for 2 minutes. Spoon the turkey filling into a 12 x 9-inch baking dish.

Top the filling with the pastry, folding the dough around the edges toward the center, and brush with the egg. Bake until the crust is deep golden brown and the filling is bubbly, about 30 minutes.

**NOTES:** *I like to simmer a turkey wing or leg with enough water to cover it by 2 inches (about 5 cups) along with ¼ cup of celery tops, carrot ends and peels, onion scraps, 4 black peppercorns, and 1 bay leaf. I let this cook down for about 30 minutes then strain the liquid into a separator, discard any excess fat, and use this as the stock for the savory filling. As with the shrimp stock I described earlier (page 101), it's great to make stocks any time and freeze for use later.*

# chicken *and* pumpkin *with* dumplings

IN KERALA, RICE FLOUR DUMPLINGS, or *pidi*, are a must for certain occasions. Like other recipes I've included in this collection, *pidi* is an item that started out as part of a religious ceremony but through the centuries became part of the culinary culture. It is often served with chicken curry at weddings and other celebrations, and it is traditional fare for guests when an expectant daughter-in-law is sent to her parents' house in her seventh month. Ladies gather around a table and roll *pidi* while discussing plans for the new baby. Here in Georgia, fans of chicken and dumplings exhibit religious fervor, but it's more of a dedication to taste than anything else, and the long-stewed chicken is served with wheat flour dumplings. Regardless of where you are from, if you like dumplings, I implore you to try this steamed cumin-seeded version made from rice flour. I use a steamer basket set over a saucepan with about two inches of water to cook the dumplings. After browning, the chicken is cooked down in coconut milk with pumpkin, ginger, bay leaf, and thyme seasoned with turmeric. Any variety of pie pumpkin or winter squash can be used in this recipe to impart the earthy sweetness. Once these chewy rice dumplings with little divots to cradle the gravy are wedded to the chicken, the dish gets a scattering of fragrant Thai basil chiffonade that is delicious enough to convert anyone!

## CHICKEN

2 tablespoons olive oil

1 small fryer chicken (2½ to 3½ pounds), cut into 8 pieces (see notes on page 73)

¼ cup unbleached all-purpose flour

3 shallots, peeled and thinly sliced

1 1-inch piece peeled fresh ginger, thinly sliced

½ of a 1-pound whole sugar pumpkin (2 cups), seeded, peeled, and diced (see notes)

2 stalks celery, rough cut into large chunks

2 fresh bay leaves

2 sprigs fresh thyme

1 teaspoon turmeric powder

1½ teaspoons salt

4 cups chicken stock

2 cups coconut milk

15 fresh Thai basil leaves (see notes)

Put the olive oil in a large Dutch oven with a tight-fitting lid and heat on medium until the oil is hot. In a separate bowl, dredge the chicken pieces in flour. Individually drop the chicken pieces into the olive oil and brown for about 2 minutes on each side. Remove the chicken from the Dutch oven. Add the shallots and ginger and cook, stirring, for 2 minutes. Add the pumpkin, celery, bay leaves, thyme, turmeric, and salt. Cook, stirring, for 1 minute; stir in the stock.

Return the chicken to the Dutch oven; cover, reduce heat to medium-low, and simmer for 15 minutes. Add the coconut milk and stir just until combined.

Drop the dumplings into the pot, stir ever so gently to coat the dumplings with the sauce, then cover again and simmer for 12 minutes.

Remove from heat. Cut the basil into chiffonade (thin ribbons), and garnish each serving with a scattering of basil.

**NOTES:** *Smaller, dense pie pumpkins work well with this recipe. However, I also like to use calabaza squash, also known as West Indian pumpkin. It has dark-green to light-orange skin mottled with amber. The only drawback in using this variety is that they grow quite large, so you will have plenty left over after making this recipe. Or try kabocha squash, or Japanese pumpkin, which has a dull, deep-green skin with some celadon to white stripes and averages about 2 to 3 pounds.*

*Thai basil has slender leaves with scalloped edges and a sweet, camphor aroma. It is native to Southeast Asia, and it possesses a distinctive flavor that is described as aniseed or licorice-like. The leaves attached to lavender-colored stems are narrower and darker than sweet basil. To cut a chiffonade, roll the leaves in a cigar-like fashion and slice into thin ribbons immediately before serving. The small threads will darken after being cut, so use them straight away.*

# DUMPLINGS

2 cups rice flour

1 teaspoon cumin seeds

1/2 teaspoon kosher salt

2 cups warm water

In a medium bowl, mix the rice flour, cumin seeds, and salt. Gradually stir in the warm water to the rice flour mixture to make a soft dough that is not sticky; the dough will have a somewhat fragile, sandy texture.

Form twenty-four 1/2-inch small balls of dough with your hands or a melon baller. Make a small divot in each dumpling by pressing down in the center with your thumb (much like making *gnocchi* or *orecchiette* pasta) and place on a plate or baking sheet.

Set a steamer basket over a medium pan with 1 quart of water; place the dumplings in the basket, making sure they are not touching, and cover. Bring the water to a boil over medium-high heat. Steam the dumplings until they are firm and plump, 8 to 10 minutes.

# fried rabbit *and* allspice bay gravy

MY MOTHER RAN A NOTORIOUSLY TIGHT SHIP IN HER KITCHENS. In Kerala, she had a cook who prepped everything, and my mother executed most of the dishes. As much as she enjoyed my being in the kitchen with her, I did not do the actual cooking. My role was more akin to that of a sous chef. When we came to America, that all changed. We no longer had additional help in the kitchen. Though I was only a teenager at the time, she decided to allow me to cook a few dishes on my own and in the process jump-started my interest and fascination with food preparation.

Typically, in a Kerala household, a daughter's role in the kitchen is largely supportive, guided by her mother. When my skills had advanced enough for my mother to trust me with preparing a whole meal, I was both nervous and excited. For my first solo meal, I chose to prepare a rabbit dish, and even after all these years, I still select rabbit for family meals. For my inaugural dish, I decided to venture away from my mother's standard and frequent rabbit curry and chose a fried-rabbit rendition. Her heartfelt after-dinner praise of my efforts remains my earliest and, perhaps, my greatest culinary triumph.

The gravy that goes along with this crispy, spiced rabbit relies on tangy buttermilk infused with allspice powder and bay.

**MAKES 4 SERVINGS**

2 cups buttermilk

1 tablespoon garlic powder

4 teaspoon sweet paprika, divided

12 whole allspice berries, ground, divided

1 1/4 teaspoons kosher salt, divided

2 dressed rabbits (2 to 2 1/2 pounds), cut into 6 to 8 pieces

2 1/2 cups canola oil, for frying

3/4 cup unbleached all-purpose flour

1/4 cup yellow cornmeal

2 teaspoons cornstarch

1/4 teaspoon baking powder

In a resealable container, combine the buttermilk, garlic powder, 2 teaspoons of the sweet paprika, 1 teaspoon of the allspice, and 3/4 teaspoon of the salt. Add the rabbit pieces, coating well with the buttermilk and spice marinade. Refrigerate, covered, for at least 8 hours and up to 12 hours.

Remove the rabbit from the marinade and drain in a colander. Discard remaining marinade.

When ready to fry the rabbit, heat the oil in a deep, heavy-bottomed skillet or Dutch oven over medium-high heat to 325°F. Set a cooling rack over a paper-towel-lined tray.

Meanwhile, in a shallow dish, combine the flour, cornmeal, cornstarch, baking powder, and the remaining paprika, allspice, and salt.

When the oil has reached frying temperature, dredge each piece of rabbit, one at a time, in the flour and cornmeal mixture, taking care to coat thoroughly. Lightly shake off excess coating before adding to the oil. Working in batches to give the rabbit plenty of room to cook and taking care to not let them touch one another, place pieces of the rabbit in the hot oil. Fry the rabbit pieces for 8 to 12 minutes, then turn over and fry until deep golden brown, about another 8 minutes. Remove the rabbit to the cooling rack. Repeat for a second batch. Pour off all but 4 tablespoons of the oil, reserving drippings in the pan, and remove any burnt chunks of cornmeal with a slotted spoon. Prepare the gravy.

## ALLSPICE BAY GRAVY

4 tablespoons of oil reserved from frying the rabbit and the drippings

4 tablespoons unbleached all-purpose flour

2 cups buttermilk

2 fresh bay leaves

1 teaspoon fresh, coarsely ground black pepper

4 whole allspice berries, ground

1/2 teaspoon kosher salt

Heat the reserved oil and drippings over medium heat in the same pan used to fry the rabbit. Sprinkle in the flour and cook while whisking constantly until the flour is lightly browned, about 1 minute. Slowly whisk in the buttermilk and cook, whisking until the gravy begins to thicken. Add the bay leaves, pepper, allspice, and salt; cook stirring often, for 4 minutes. The gravy will be quite thick, so if needed, thin by whisking in a bit more buttermilk. Serve the gravy alongside the fried rabbit.

# down south goat biryani

*BIRYANI* IS A CELEBRATION DISH. Weddings, birthdays, festivals, and other times of good cheer are the usual occasions when this iconic dish of rice with meat or vegetables graces our table, with almost the entire spice cabinet having been invited into the cooking vessel. Across India, Pakistan, Bangladesh, Sri Lanka, and Malaysia, countless renditions of this festive dinner abound, as do the many names by which it is known.

When I was twenty-four years old, my brother Joy got married, and we all went to India for the wedding. This was my first experience eating *biryani* as prepared by a "real" *biryani* chef. In India, traveling *biryani* chefs, much like the BBQ pit masters here in the United States, have been cooking this time-honored dish at gatherings for generations. Often at Indian weddings, these chefs are hired to come and pitch tents in the backyard to cook their famous *biryani* for hundreds or, as in my brother's case, upward of a thousand guests. Observing a masterful chef prepare the *biryani* that day was nothing short of awe inspiring. I watched the process like a hawk, observing every detail that went into making this traditional fare for the large crowd attending the wedding. The goats were bought live, butchered on the property, and broken down specifically for this meal. The huge cooking pots could easily have accommodated a couple of adults. Two assistant chefs maneuvered the gigantic cauldrons over wood fires built on a bed of coal and sand in the yard. I do believe the spectacle of a traveling *biryani* chef and his crew coupled with my dear brother's nuptials made this wedding the most memorable one I've ever attended. Having often observed as my mother and other relatives make *biryani* for birthdays and special holidays, I can truly say I learned how to make this dish on my brother's wedding day.

I think the following recipe is my favorite version to make at home, though it is wonderful made with beef chuck roast or chicken thighs. I love the tender goat layered between saffron-spiced rice and baked, then dressed with roasted shallots, cashews, raisins, and a confetti of cilantro.

As I fluff the flavored rice, I always remove the star anise, cardamom pods, cinnamon sticks, cloves, and bay leaves—counting the fifteen spice hulls as I go—and set them aside to use as a garnish. Alternatively, you can tie all the spices except the saffron and cumin seeds in a piece of muslin to make a bouquet garni, which makes a quick job of removing the spice hulls. Or, if no muslin is available, put them in a tea ball and hang the ball over the side of the pot.

## RICE

6 green cardamom pods, crushed

2 black cardamom pods, crushed

4 garlic cloves, thinly sliced

2 star anise

2 sticks cinnamon (about 6 inches total)

3 fresh bay leaves

15 threads saffron

1 teaspoon cumin seed

2 teaspoons kosher salt

3 tablespoons ghee

3 cups basmati rice

In a 3-quart pot with $4\frac{1}{2}$ cups of water, add the cardamom, cloves, star anise, cinnamon, and bay leaves and bring to a simmer, covered, over low heat. Add the saffron, cumin, salt, and ghee; increase heat and bring to a rolling boil. Add the rice, stir briefly, then cover tightly; reduce heat to low and cook for 12 minutes—making sure to not lift the lid—until the liquid is absorbed. Remove from heat and let sit, covered, for 10 minutes. Fluff with a fork and set aside. Remove the spice hulls, using one of the methods suggested in the recipe description, page 186.

## GOAT

2 bunches fresh cilantro (2 cups), leaves and stems, chopped

1 cup mint leaves

2 serrano chiles, slit in half lengthwise

6 garlic cloves

3 tablespoons peeled, chopped fresh ginger

3 tablespoons ghee

2 large red onions, peeled, halved, and thinly sliced (about 1½ cups)

1 tablespoon garam masala

1 teaspoon green cardamom powder

1½ teaspoons kosher salt

1 goat leg (3 pounds), cut into 1-inch pieces (see notes)

In a blender or food processor, combine 1 cup water with the cilantro, mint, chiles, garlic, and ginger. Blend the ingredients to make a thick paste; set it aside.

In a large Dutch oven, heat the ghee over medium-high heat. Add the onions and cook, stirring often, until the onions are golden brown, about 8 minutes. Add the garam masala, cardamom powder, and salt; cook and stir for 1 minute. Add the herb paste, and stir until well combined. Lower the heat and cook the sauce for 3 minutes. Add the goat and stir to coat all the meat with the sauce. Cover and cook until the meat is falling off the bone, about 45 minutes to an hour.

**NOTE:** *Have your butcher cut the meat into small pieces.*

## GARNISH

3 shallots, skin on, cut in half lengthwise

2 garlic bulbs, skin on, cut in half crosswise

2 tablespoons ghee, melted, divided

1/2 cup cashews

1/2 cup golden raisins

1/2 cup chopped cilantro (for garnish after assembling the dish)

Place the shallots and garlic in a small pan and drizzle with 1 tablespoon of the melted ghee. Roast the shallots and garlic for 20 minutes, while the goat is cooking.

In a separate pan, heat 1 tablespoon ghee and toast the cashews and raisins until golden brown, about 2 minutes.

## ASSEMBLING *the* BIRYANI

Heat the oven to 350°F.

In a roasting pan, layer one-third of the rice, then top the rice with one-half of the goat; repeat and end with a layer of rice. Cover the pan tightly with foil.

Bake until all the flavors of the rice and goat combine, about 20 minutes. Uncover and garnish with reserved spice hulls. When ready to serve the *biryani*, place the roasted shallots, garlic, cashews, and raisins on top of the rice. Sprinkle with the cilantro.

# sunday beef stew

DURING MY CHILDHOOD, weekends customarily began with the butcher's arrival in town each Saturday morning. My mother would purchase beef, rub it down with black pepper and turmeric, and then set it to rest in preparation for a big Sunday night family gathering. This familiar stew of chuck roast, potatoes, garlic, and pearl onions is uniquely seasoned with fresh ginger and serrano chiles in rich coconut milk.

3 tablespoons canola oil, divided

1½ pounds beef chuck, cut into 1-inch pieces

1 teaspoon fresh coarsely ground black peppercorns plus more for seasoning

1 teaspoon kosher salt plus more for seasoning

5 garlic cloves, chopped

3 serrano chiles, seeded and chopped

1 1 x 1-inch piece peeled fresh ginger, thinly sliced

1 teaspoon turmeric, ground

3 cups low-salt beef stock

½ pound small carrots, scrubbed or peeled, halved lengthwise

½ pound baby red-skinned potatoes, halved, or quartered if large

¼ pound fresh or frozen red pearl onions, peeled and halved

2 cups coconut milk

Heat 1½ tablespoons of the oil in a large heavy pot over medium-high heat. Season the beef with salt and pepper. Working in two batches and adding and heating the remaining 1½ tablespoons of oil between batches, add the beef and sear, turning occasionally, until browned on all sides, about 5 minutes. Transfer the beef to a plate.

Stir in the garlic, chiles, and ginger and cook, stirring often, until very fragrant, about 2 minutes. Add 1 teaspoon of the pepper, 1 teaspoon of the salt, and the turmeric; cook, stirring constantly until fragrant, for 1 minute. Add the stock and reserved beef with any accumulated juices. Bring to a boil, scraping up any browned bits from the bottom of pot. Reduce heat to medium low, cover, and simmer, stirring occasionally, until the beef is tender, about 45 minutes.

Add the carrots, potatoes, and onions. Cover and simmer, stirring occasionally, until vegetables are tender, 15 to 20 minutes. Stir in the coconut milk and remove from heat. Serve immediately.

**NOTES:** *In our home, the beef would be cooked the night before, and the dish finished right when we arrived back home from Mass on Sundays. With the meat precooked, only vegetables and coconut needed to be added, reducing cooking time the day the stew was served.*

# country ham
# smothered cabbage

MY AWAKENING TO THE WONDERS OF COUNTRY HAM has been one of the delights of living in my American South. Country ham is a variety of dry-cured ham that uses a salt-and-smoke-curing method ubiquitous to rural parts of the Deep South. The meat is not cooked but rather preserved by the smoke, which turns the meat a deep reddish color. Country ham is often sold whole, bone-in, and unrefrigerated in rough cotton bags. City dwellers sometimes liken the flavor to that of Italy's famed *prosciutto crudo* or Spain's *jambon iberico*. The difference, however, lies in the fact that authentic country hams are always hardwood smoked, usually using hickory or red oak fires. The smoking process imparts a distinctive and subtle flavor complexity not found in other dry-cured hams.

In this soulfully satisfying dinner, wedges of cabbage are smothered in gravy with leeks, nutmeg, and chili flakes and roasted, then the dish is drizzled with mustard-tempered coconut oil.

1 large head of cabbage

2 teaspoons kosher salt, divided

4 tablespoons (1/2 stick) unsalted butter

2 large leeks, thinly sliced and rinsed

1 green bell pepper, seeded and diced

1/4 pound hickory smoked country ham, cut into 1/4-inch pieces

2 garlic cloves, finely chopped

1/4 cup unbleached all-purpose flour

2 cups buttermilk

1 teaspoon freshly grated nutmeg

1 teaspoon crushed red pepper flakes

1 tablespoon coconut oil

1 teaspoon brown mustard seeds

Heat the oven to 375°F. Spray a 13 x 9-inch pan with cooking spray and set aside.

Stand the cabbage on its stem end. Cut it in half, then cut each half of the cabbage into four wedges, making eight wedges total, taking care to make sure each wedge is held together with a section of the core so that the wedges stay in nice pieces while cooking.

In a large pot, place 1 teaspoon of the salt and the cabbage wedges, add enough water to cover the cabbage, and then bring to a boil over high heat. Cover, reduce heat to low, and cook the cabbage until it is just tender, about 10 minutes. Drain the cabbage in a colander and place in the prepared baking dish.

In a large skillet over medium-low heat, melt the butter. Add the leeks and bell pepper and cook, stirring occasionally, until the leeks are tender, about 5 minutes. Add the ham and garlic and cook, stirring, for 3 minutes or until the garlic is tender. Add the flour and cook, stirring constantly, for 1 minute, taking care to break up any lumps of flour.

Gradually stir in the buttermilk. Cook, stirring constantly until the gravy is thick and bubbly, about 2 minutes. Add the remaining salt, nutmeg, and red pepper flakes and stir well.

Pour the gravy over the cabbage and bake until the cabbage is roasted and tender and the gravy is thickened and creamy, about 20 minutes.

In a small saucepan, temper the coconut oil by heating it over high heat until hot then reduce to medium. Add the mustard seeds and toast until the seeds begin to pop, about 30 seconds.

Drizzle the tempered oil and mustard seeds over the cabbage and serve at once.

# gilded acorn squash *with* coconut milk rice *and* golden pepper sauce

AT MY MOTHER'S ELBOW, I carefully observed and learned to prepare many different recipes using squash, gourds, and cucumbers. A myriad of squash varieties are a fundamental ingredient in Indian cuisine. But acorn squash, indigenous to North and Central America, is a relatively new addition to my repertoire. This lovely dark green species with its characteristic single splotch of orange or yellow is commonly available year-round, although it is considered a winter vegetable. As the name suggests, it resembles an acorn—that is if an acorn weighed a couple of pounds! In this recipe, acorn squash is roasted with cane syrup, cinnamon, nutmeg, and butter, filled with Coconut Milk Rice, and draped with a golden pepper and coconut cream sauce.

**MAKES 6 SERVINGS**

3 medium acorn squash, halved lengthwise and seeded

6 tablespoons (3/4 stick) unsalted butter, divided

3 tablespoons cane syrup, divided

1/2 teaspoon nutmeg, freshly grated

1/2 teaspoon cinnamon powder

1 teaspoon kosher salt

Heat the oven to 400°F. Line a large rimmed baking sheet with parchment paper or foil.

Place the squash cut-side up on the baking sheet and place 1 tablespoon of butter and 1 1/2 teaspoons of the cane syrup in each squash half. Sprinkle with nutmeg, cinnamon, and salt. Bake until very tender when tested with a fork, about 1 hour.

In the meantime, begin preparing Coconut Milk Rice.

## COCONUT MILK RICE

2 tablespoons coconut oil

1 teaspoon cumin seeds

3 green cardamom pods, crushed

1 teaspoon kosher salt

1½ cups coconut milk

2 cups white basmati rice

In a 2-quart pot, over medium heat, heat the coconut oil until it is hot. Add the cumin seeds and cardamom and cook for 30 seconds. Add the salt, coconut milk, 1½ cups water, and rice. Stir well and bring to a boil uncovered. Lower heat to low, cover tightly, and cook, making sure to not lift the lid, for 12 minutes, or until liquid is absorbed. Remove from heat and let stand, covered, for 10 minutes. Fluff the rice with a fork.

To assemble the dish, place each squash half with a serving of rice. Fill the squash with the Golden Pepper Sauce.

## GOLDEN PEPPER SAUCE

2 tablespoons canola oil

½ teaspoon black mustard seeds

2 medium shallots, peeled and thinly sliced

2 medium thinly sliced yellow bell peppers (about 1 cup)

1 teaspoon kosher salt

1 teaspoon turmeric powder

1½ cups coconut milk

In a medium skillet, over medium-high heat, heat the canola oil and add the mustard seeds and shallots. Cook and stir until the shallots are tender, about 3 minutes. Add the peppers and salt; reduce heat to medium and cook, stirring often, until the peppers are semisoft, about 2 minutes. Add the turmeric and stir well. Add the coconut milk, increase heat to medium high, and bring the sauce to a quick boil. Remove the sauce from the heat.

# vivid tomato *and* cheese pie

VISUALLY STUNNING, this summer showstopper is my favorite recipe for entertaining during the peak of tomato season. Guests swoon at the sight and sigh with delight at the taste of this simple ricotta and manchego pie in a flaky cream cheese crust. Chives and parsley give flavorful support to the ripe tomatoes without overpowering them. The sharp bite of black pepper matches the creamy cheese, and the display of this dish's colorful tomatoes shouts summer. It doesn't matter whether in Kerala or Kennesaw, tables draped with a brightly colored madras cloth adorned with this bright tomato pie as the centerpiece is summer party perfection.

The crust for this pie is "blind baked," a process of making a piecrust without the filling. In this instance, the crust is partially baked, filled, and then baked again. I like to use a small, easy to remove chain weight to keep the crust's bottom from rising, but rice also works well.

## VIVID TOMATO and CHEESE PIE

2¹/2 pounds heirloom tomatoes, thickly sliced

¹/2 of Cream Cheese Piecrust (page 39), rolled to ¹/8 inch thick and cut into a 12-inch circle

2¹/2 cups ricotta cheese, drained in a colander

2 large eggs, beaten

1¹/2 cups grated manchego cheese

3 tablespoons panko breadcrumbs

2 teaspoons very finely chopped garlic

2 tablespoons chopped fresh chives

2 tablespoons chopped fresh parsley leaves

2 teaspoons fresh coarsely ground black peppercorns, divided

1 teaspoon crushed red pepper flakes, divided

1¹/2 teaspoons kosher salt, divided

1 tablespoon olive oil

Heat the oven to 350°F. Place the tomatoes in a colander to drain for 30 minutes, tossing occasionally. Reserve the juice for later use, if desired.

Line a 9-inch cast-iron skillet or deep-dish pie pan with the dough and prick the bottom of the crust several times with a fork to keep it from puffing up while baking. Line the dough with parchment paper. Place pie weights or rice over the bottom and up the sides of the paper. Bake until edges are beginning to brown, about 15 minutes. Remove the paper and weights and return to the oven to bake until the interior crust is light golden, about 10 minutes. Place the piecrust in the skillet or pan on a rack to cool.

Meanwhile, in a medium bowl, combine the ricotta, egg, manchego, breadcrumbs, garlic, chives, parsley, 1 teaspoon of the black pepper, ¹/2 teaspoon of the red pepper flakes, and 1 teaspoon of salt.

Evenly spread the cheese mixture into the crust. Arrange the tomatoes over the cheese. Sprinkle the remaining pepper, red pepper flakes, and salt over the tomatoes. Drizzle with the olive oil. Bake the pie until the tomatoes are browned, about 45 minutes. Place the pie on a rack to cool for at least 20 minutes before slicing to serve.

# clove baked sweet potatoes

THIS IS A "SNUGGLE" DISH. Curl up on the couch with a bowl of these *beurre noisette* and clove roasted sweet potatoes, breathe a sigh of relief, and relax as the fragrant steam wafts up and fills the air. As the nutty, lip-licking lusciousness of the browned butter collides with the warming sensation of the cloves and sets your tongue a-tingling, you will know immediately that it is time to hunker down.

4 large sweet potatoes, halved lengthwise

8 tablespoons browned butter, divided (see notes)

3/4 teaspoon kosher salt

1/2 teaspoon clove powder, divided

1 tablespoon plus 1 1/2 teaspoons packed dark-brown sugar

Heat the oven to 400°F. Line a rimmed baking sheet with parchment paper or foil.

Cut each sweet potato half with a crosshatch pattern in the flesh or cut side using a sharp paring knife and place on the lined baking sheet cut-side up. Rub 1 1/2 teaspoons of the browned butter on the cut sides of each sweet potato half. Sprinkle the butter with salt and 1/4 teaspoon of the clove powder. Bake until the sweet potatoes are fork-tender, about 35 minutes.

Meanwhile, combine the remaining browned butter, the remaining clove powder, and brown sugar, and keep warm.

When the sweet potatoes are tender, transfer to serving bowls and drizzle the sweetened brown butter over the sweet potatoes. Serve warm.

**NOTES:** *To make browned butter, over medium heat melt unsalted butter in a light-colored pan—so you can see the color changing as it browns. As the butter melts, it will begin to foam. When the foaming subsides, the color will change from lemony yellow to golden, then to tan, and finally a deep nutty brown. Once you smell the nutty aroma and the butter is browned, remove from heat and transfer to a heatproof bowl and allow to cool. Browned butter will keep refrigerated for several months. Ghee is very slightly browned. This butter is much darker.*

# roasted garlicky potato salad

THIS IS ONE OF THOSE DISHES that works well at any family gathering, potluck, or picnic. My Ethan and I love having picnics. Many afternoons before I pick him up from after-school activities, I pack a little picnic basket with a sandwich and this potato salad. Lemon juice keeps the flavors bright, and garlic and serrano peppers ratchet up the dressing.

After school we'll park the car and walk to Chandler Park across the street from his school, with a picnic basket, a Frisbee, and a book or two in tow. We find the perfect tree, which in itself is a process in a fifty-five-acre park. We sit under our tree, lay out our picnic blanket on the grass, and talk about how our day has been thus far. He might climb up into the tree's branches or throw the Frisbee while I unpack the food basket, or we might just sprawl out on the blanket and read awhile. I love my time with Ethan, every precious moment of it. My son is at an age now where he is no longer a little kid. He loves a good conversation, and I adore listening to his opinions and insights.

4 tablespoons extra-virgin olive oil

3 tablespoons fresh lemon juice

2 garlic cloves, finely chopped

4 serrano chiles, seeded and finely chopped

1 teaspoon kosher salt

1½ pounds small gold potatoes, washed, skin on, cut into 1-inch pieces

½ cup mayonnaise

1 teaspoon very finely chopped garlic

Zest of 3 lemons

¼ cup chopped fresh flat-leaf parsley, leaves only

**MAKES 6 SERVINGS**

Heat the oven to 375°F. In a large bowl, whisk together the olive oil, lemon juice, minced garlic, serrano chiles, and salt. Add the potatoes to the mixture, and toss to coat the potatoes evenly with the olive oil mixture. Transfer to a rimmed baking sheet and roast the potatoes for 25 to 30 minutes, or until golden brown and cooked through. Check on the potatoes every 10 minutes and stir them around. Remove from the oven and transfer back into the large bowl. Add the mayonnaise, garlic, lemon zest, and parsley and toss until the roasted potatoes are evenly coated. Serve at room temperature or cold.

# red pepper flake brussels sprouts pachadi

*PACHADI* REFERS TO A TRADITIONAL SOUTH INDIAN SIDE DISH. The definition of the word *pachadi* is quite different among the many different regions of southern India. To the east in Andhra Pradesh, *pachadi* is analogous to pickles that are preserved for several months. In Kerala and Tamil Nadu, however, *pachadi* is typically made of varying types of vegetables with green or red chiles tempered in oil with mustard seeds dressed with yogurt. This rendition featuring Brussels sprouts is so popular we can easily go through 20 pounds of the little green orbs per day at Spice to Table.

**MAKES 6 SERVINGS**

1½ pounds (about 36) Brussels sprouts, trimmed and halved end to end (see notes)

3 tablespoons olive oil

1 teaspoon brown mustard seeds

1¼ teaspoons crushed red pepper flakes

2 teaspoons peeled, finely chopped fresh ginger

1½ teaspoons kosher salt, divided

1 cup (8 ounces) plain Greek-style yogurt

1 teaspoon very finely chopped garlic

Heat the oven to 400°F.

In a large bowl, toss the Brussels sprouts with the oil, mustard seeds, pepper flakes, ginger, and ¾ teaspoon of the salt. Using your hands, make sure the seasonings get into every nook and cranny of the sprouts. Pour the coated sprouts onto a baking sheet, scraping any leftover seasoning in the bowl onto the sprouts. Roast the sprouts until golden brown, about 30 minutes.

Meanwhile, in a medium bowl, whisk the yogurt, garlic, and remaining salt until it is creamy, about 1 minute. When the sprouts are roasted to a golden hue, drizzle the whipped yogurt over the Brussels sprouts and serve at once.

**NOTES:** *In the most of the United States, late September through February is the best time to purchase Brussels sprouts. Choose sprouts with tight, compact heads that feel hard when gently squeezed. Look for uniform color with no puffiness, yellowed leaves, or ends. Brussels sprouts are best when bought still on the stem, and the smaller ones are sweeter, but those found loose or prepackaged are almost as good. When anyone proclaims they don't like sprouts, change their minds with this dish.*

# creamed spinach *with* fresh mozzarella

I'VE ALWAYS LOVED SPINACH, be it a southern creamed spinach or a northern Indian *palak* (spinach) *paneer* (Indian cheese). This recipe brings these two dishes together with a twist, using small balls of fresh mozzarella called *bocconcini* instead of *paneer*. When the cheese is warmed through, the seasoned spinach is spooned over basmati rice, making a dish hearty enough for a vegetarian entrée.

6 tablespoons olive oil, divided

1 large red onion, roughly chopped (about 1 cup)

1 tablespoon very finely chopped garlic

1 tablespoon peeled, grated fresh ginger

2 dried red chile peppers, broken

2 teaspoons cumin powder

1 tablespoon coriander powder

1 teaspoon turmeric powder

1$^1$/2 teaspoons kosher salt

3 pounds fresh spinach, stemmed and torn

1/2 cup chopped cilantro leaves and stems

3/4 cup sour cream

8 ounces fresh mozzarella cut into 1-inch pieces or bocconcini

4 cups cooked white basmati rice

**MAKES 4 SERVINGS**

In a large saucepan over medium heat, add 3 tablespoons of olive oil. Add the onion and cook until the onion is golden brown, about 6 minutes. Add the garlic, ginger, and dried red chiles and cook for 1 minute, stirring constantly. Add the cumin, coriander, turmeric, and salt and stir for another minute. Add the spinach, handfuls at a time, and cook until it is cooked down, about 10 minutes. Remove from the heat and allow to cool slightly. Pour the spinach mixture into a food processor or blender and add the cilantro. Blend for 15 to 30 seconds, or until puréed. Heat the remaining olive oil in the saucepan, pour the spinach mixture back into the pan, and simmer over low heat for 10 minutes, or until the spinach purée bubbles like molten lava. Fold in the sour cream and add the mozzarella. Reduce the heat to low and simmer for 1 minute to soften the cheese. Serve warm over rice.

# red cabbage thoren

KERALA CUISINE IS KNOWN FOR QUICK STIR-FRIES. The trinity, or starting base, for many, many dishes cooked in Kerala is coconut oil, curry leaves, and mustard seeds. The scents that permeate most kitchens in Kerala are from combinations of these ingredients as they perform their magic in the cooking pan. Here's a quick stir-fry of red cabbage and grated fresh coconut. I love the mustard and curry bite of this cabbage stir-fry served along with Black Cardamom Smothered Pork Chop (page 78). Because of its versatility, this is a staple dish in my cooking classes at Third Space. This recipe calls for red cabbage, but I'd be remiss if I didn't tell you it is wonderful with summer squash, carrots, romanesco, or okra, just to name a few. It's a quick stir-fry freckled with shredded coconut.

**MAKES 4 TO 6 SERVINGS**

2 tablespoons canola oil

1 teaspoon brown mustard seeds

1 teaspoon cumin seed

10 fresh curry leaves or 2 fresh bay leaves

1 red cabbage (2 pounds or 8 cups), cored and coarsely chopped

1/2 teaspoon turmeric powder

1/2 teaspoon kosher salt

4 garlic cloves, thinly sliced

1 serrano chile, seeded and chopped

1 cup fresh grated coconut

Over medium-high heat, heat the oil. Add the mustard seeds and stir for 30 seconds or until the seeds begin to pop. Add the cumin and curry leaves and cook until fragrant, about 30 seconds. Add the cabbage, turmeric, and salt. Cook stirring occasionally, until the cabbage is crisp tender, about 3 minutes. Add 1/2 cup of water and cook until the cabbage is tender and the water has evaporated, 5 to 6 minutes. Discard the bay leaves, if using.

Meanwhile, in a mini food processor or blender, combine the garlic, chiles, coconut, and 1/4 cup of water. Pulse to form a paste. Scrape the paste into the cabbage and toss to coat the cabbage. Cook and stir for an additional 2 minutes. Serve at once or at room temperature.

**NOTES:** *If exposed to the least bit of alkaline conditions (like hard water), red cabbage will turn slate blue. To revive the color, should your cabbage begin to turn blue, quickly add 1 tablespoon lemon juice or cider vinegar.*

# pineapple mango raita

MANY VIEW *RAITA* as a condiment, but it serves a much higher purpose. *Raita* doesn't merely add flavor to food, it actually enhances the flavor of any dish served with it. This recipe eschews vegetables for sweet mango and pineapple, but it retains the spicy yet cooling effect of other versions. The sweet, tart fruit combined with hot chiles suspended in a cooling yogurt that is punctuated with tempered mustard and cumin oil pairs phenomenally with Country Captain (page 71) or Railways Beef Curry (page 94).

A clever cook prepares all the ingredients for this mustard-seed-infused fruit *raita* ahead of time and stirs them together right before serving.

2 cups plain Greek-style yogurt

1/2 teaspoon kosher salt

1 tablespoon white granulated sugar

1 small to medium fresh pineapple, trimmed, cored, and cut into 1/4-inch pieces or frozen pineapple chunks, thawed (2 cups)

1 medium ripe fresh mango, peeled and cut into 1/4-inch pieces or frozen mango pieces, thawed (1 cup)

2 serrano chiles, seeded and finely chopped

2 tablespoons canola oil

1/2 teaspoon brown mustard seeds

1/2 teaspoon cumin seeds

**MAKES 6 SERVINGS**

In a medium bowl, combine the yogurt, salt, sugar, pineapple, mango, and chiles.

In a small saucepan over medium-high heat, heat the oil; add the mustard and cumin seeds and cook until seeds begin to pop, about 30 seconds. Fold the oil and seeds into the yogurt and fruit. Serve immediately or within 1 hour, as it will separate over time.

# quick pickled peaches

I LOVE THE VARIETY OF NAMES OF GEORGIA PEACHES as much as I love the variety of flavors. Spring Prince, Rich Lady, and Southern Pearl are a few of those special names. One of my favorite preparations is this quick pickle. Fish sauce adds a deep umami flavor that is hard to pinpoint. Far from tasting fishy, these peaches have deep sweet and savory spice with the crunch of quickly pickled pearl onions. Nectarines, apricots, and cherries are great treated with this same pickling method. Serve these pickled peaches with Goat Confit Sliders (page 86), Masala Lamb Burgers (page 88), or Chervil Lime Lobster Salad Roll (page 91).

MAKES 6 SERVINGS

4 to 6 large firm ripe peaches (about 1 pound)

Ice bath, for peaches

1/2 cup apple cider vinegar

1/4 cup fish sauce

1/2 cup white granulated sugar

10 whole cloves

3 whole star anise

1/4 teaspoon kosher salt

1/2 cup peeled pearl onions or green onions (white bulb only)

Cut a shallow x in the bottom of each peach with a paring knife.

In a 4-quart pot, boil 2½ quarts of water; add the peaches and blanch 10 to 15 seconds. Transfer the peaches to a bowl of cold water and ice, and let stand until cool enough to handle. Peel peaches, then halve lengthwise and pit.

In a 2-quart pot over medium-high heat, add ½ cup of water, vinegar, fish sauce, sugar, cloves, star anise, and salt; bring to a boil. Add the peaches and onions and let sit for 1 to 2 hours at room temperature. Place the peaches in a jar and add enough of the hot pickling liquid to cover.

Cover and refrigerate until ready to serve.

# desserts & sweets

*I suspect I may have been a fruit bat in a former life. I seem to be genetically predisposed to be drawn to any sort of fruit, especially mangoes.*

In Kerala, cooks are blessed with a bounty of locally harvested fresh fruit, and many meals conclude with a fruited dessert. Here in the southern United States, I have become enamored with sweet, juicy Georgia peaches, Virginia apples, Louisiana strawberries, Florida oranges, and Texas grapefruit—plus the melons of every sort harvested from just about every state. And oh my, the pecans! While peanuts are virtually universal, pecans are still considered a Deep South delicacy. The most bountiful, lusciously buttery, and meaty pecans are harvested each fall all across the region. I have become a fan of all types of pies and tall southern layer cakes. I grew up on sweet puddings and dark spiced toffees. So you see, both of my two Souths appeal to the sweetest of sweet tooths—my own. These desserts range from simple to elaborate, but even pastry beginners and novice bakers can master these desserts. After all, to nourish is to nurture—and nurturing is the sweetest thing of all.

# ethan's bespoke frozen bananas

LIKE HIS MOM, MY SON HAS A SWEET TOOTH and is he ever keen on chocolate. Hoping to limit his chocolate intake while encouraging him to eat lots of fruit, I was happy to discover chocolate-covered bananas when he was really young. Over the years, I began making these frozen delights at home, and the toppings have evolved from rainbow sprinkles and chocolate jimmies to much healthier options—often at his suggestion. In this version, we use cashews and coconut shreds to turn what was once a sugar-laden snack into a nutritious and satisfying source of quick energy, protein, and potassium. When I make these at home, they are his and his alone—I am lucky to sneak one for myself when he's at school. I try to keep popsicle sticks handy to whip up a batch when I have a few extra bananas. I find cutting the tips off the bananas gives a bit more surface area for the sprinkles.

**MAKES 6 FROZEN TREATS**

3 bananas, peeled and cut in half widthwise, tips removed

1 cup (8 ounces) semisweet chocolate, chopped

1 tablespoon unsalted butter

1/2 cup (4 ounces) salted roasted cashews, coarsely chopped

1/2 cup sweetened shredded coconut

Insert a stick or skewer in one end of each banana, about 3 inches. Place the bananas on a sheet pan lined with parchment paper and freeze for 15 minutes.

In a double boiler or heatproof bowl set over a pan of gently simmering water, add the shaved semisweet chocolate and butter. Stir gently with a spatula until melted.

Remove the bananas from the freezer and dip them in the chocolate, coating them evenly.

Sprinkle the bananas with the roasted cashews and shredded coconut, and set on the lined sheet pan. Place in the freezer for 10 minutes, or until the chocolate is set.

**NOTES:** *Once the chocolate is set, wrap each banana individually in plastic wrap for a quick answer to the "home from school" treat question every mother knows so well.*

*For a different kind of flavorful crunch, try finely chopped pecans instead of cashews, or if tree nut allergies are a concern, substitute shelled salted pumpkin (pepitas) or sunflower seeds. Crushed-up cereal or granola are super additions, too.*

# almond *and* pear brioche pudding

FOLKS IN THE DEEP SOUTH are oh-so-familiar with the kind of comforting goodness that comes from mixing some day-old bread soaked in milk with eggs, sugar, and spices and baking the mixture in the oven. My favorite part of this baked pudding is the way the bread crusts peek out through the custard, crisply browned and all sugary and nutty with sliced almonds. Another delightful surprise are the little glistening jewels of ripe Bosc pears, enrobed in the delicate almond and cardamom custard.

2 tablespoons unsalted butter, softened

1 cup white granulated sugar, divided

1/3 cup sliced raw almonds

6 large eggs

1 teaspoon green cardamom powder

1 1/2 teaspoons pure almond extract

1 cup whole milk

1 cup heavy cream

4 to 5 slices day-old brioche bread (about 4 cups), cut into 1-inch cubes

2 Bosc pears, peeled, cored, and cut into 1/2-inch pieces (see notes)

Jaggery Cumin Drizzle (page 260)

MAKES 6 TO 8 SERVINGS

Heat the oven to 350°F. Grease a 9-inch round cake pan with the softened butter.

Mix 2 tablespoons of the sugar with the almond slices and set aside while mixing the pudding.

Whisk the eggs in a large bowl until well mixed. Add the cardamom powder, almond extract, and remaining sugar, and whisk to combine. Whisk in the milk and heavy cream until well combined. Add the bread and the pears, and stir to incorporate. Pour the mixture into the prepared cake pan. Sprinkle the top of the pudding with the sugar and almond slices. Bake until the pudding is set and puffy and the top is golden, about 40 to 45 minutes. Let cool somewhat, then serve warm or at room temperature, drizzled with the spiced jaggery sauce.

**NOTES:** *Bosc pears have fat bottoms and long necks. These pears have a brassy brown skin that does not change color as it ripens. They are used in this recipe because Bosc pears have enough body density to stand up well during baking. For tips on selecting and ripening pears, see notes on page 221.*

# tarragon-laced apricot compote

PEOPLE IN MY TWO SOUTHS AGREE that few desserts equal a fresh fruit compote. It is easy to prepare with no dairy ingredients. For centuries in virtually every region of the world, slow-cooked fruits in syrups, or compotes, have ended meals in households high and low. This apricot compote is delicious on its own served warm or chilled, spooned over a simple, classic pound cake, or used as a topping for ice cream. The possibilities are virtually endless for serving this compote; you will have fun discovering and creating your own ideas for it.

5 to 8 ripe apricots (1 pound), halved and pitted

Zest and juice of 1 Meyer lemon

3 tablespoons white granulated sugar

1/2 teaspoon fresh coarsely ground black peppercorns

1/4 teaspoon kosher salt

1 teaspoon fresh tarragon leaves

Combine the apricots, Meyer lemon zest and juice, sugar, black pepper, and salt in a large skillet. Cook over medium heat, flipping the apricots once halfway through cooking, until the fruit is glazed and very tender, about 8 to 10 minutes. Transfer to a small bowl and fold in the tarragon. Serve warm or cold.

**NOTES:** *Any stone fruit—peaches, plums, nectarines, or cherries—cooked in a compote this way is very tasty. Try some of the newer apricot-plum hybrids—pluots, plumcots, apriums, or apriplums—in this recipe.*

# watermelon thai basil granita

THIS REFRESHING, SWEET, and savory shaved-ice dessert is perfect for the last course of a summer patio supper. Try either yellow-fleshed or ripe juicy red watermelon in this lime and basil slushy for grown-ups.

1/2 (about 6 cups) medium seedless watermelon flesh, cut into 2-inch pieces

1 cup (8 ounces) honey

1/2 cup (1/2 ounce) fresh Thai basil leaves, stemmed, plus a few for garnish

1 teaspoon fresh lime zest

1 tablespoon fresh lime juice

1/2 teaspoon kosher salt

MAKES 6 SERVINGS

In a blender or food processor add the watermelon, honey, Thai basil, lime zest, lime juice, and salt to a food processor and blend on high until smooth.

Pour the mixture into a 12 x 9-inch nonstick metal baking pan. Place the pan in the freezer and freeze for 30 minutes. Remove from the freezer and, using a fork, stir icy portions into the middle of the pan. Place it back in the freezer and repeat two more times. Remove from the freezer and scrape the granita into flaky crystals, using a fork. Cover tightly and freeze. Scrape the granita into martini glasses, garnish with Thai basil leaves, and serve with a demitasse spoon.

# pink peppercorn *and* ginger poached pears

ALTHOUGH INDIA RECEIVED PEARS FROM CHINA many centuries ago, and they are grown and available most commonly in the northern provinces, they are still not nearly as beloved a fruit as the mango. In the southern US, pears struggle to compete with peaches, which are harvested regionally about the same time in the summer and into the fall. But when it comes to poaching—and I love poaching all types of fruit—the pear seems to be the best fruit, with its ability to retain its shape and its blossoming flavor. Because of importation and advanced agricultural practices, lovely ripe pears are available at the grocery store at almost any time of the year. However, for this recipe I chose a darling little pear called Seckel, also known as a sugar pear, because it is unrivaled in terms of sweetness. With a short, round, chubby appearance, sugar pears offer an off-white to pale yellow flesh that is slightly more dense and coarse than other varieties; they embody the phrase "good things come in small packages." Seckel pears—or many other varieties for that matter, such as Bosc, Anjou, or Bartlett—are perfect for this dessert since they readily absorb the flavors and fragrance of the ginger and sweet pink peppercorns. Serve these pears with Macaroon Drops (page 258) for a stunning fall dessert.

## PINK PEPPERCORN *and* GINGER POACHED PEARS

1 cup white granulated sugar

2 tablespoons peeled, grated fresh ginger

2 teaspoons dried pink peppercorns (see notes)

10 strands of saffron

6 Seckel pears, peeled, stems attached

In a 3-quart pot, over medium heat, bring 4 cups of water with the sugar, ginger, peppercorns, and saffron to a boil. Add the pears, reduce heat to low, and simmer, occasionally basting the pears, until the liquid is reduced by one-half and has reached a syrupy consistency and the pears are tender when lightly pierced with a sharp knife tip, about 20 to 25 minutes.

Serve the pears drizzled with the remaining warm syrup.

**NOTES:** *Pink peppercorns are not really peppercorns at all; they are the dried berries from either a member of the rose family commonly known as the Peruvian peppertree or a related species known as the Brazilian pepper. They are so named because not only do they look like peppercorns, but they also have a peppery taste. Pink peppercorns release a faintly pine-like aroma and have a sweet, warming scent. I think these rosy peppercorns give off just the right amount of heat and wed beautifully with the warm ginger to create a new flavor for poached pears.*

When buying pears for immediate use, test for ripeness by slightly pressing the skin near the stem. It should feel slightly soft, but the body of the pear should be firm. If a pear feels soft all over, it is generally overripe, and the flesh may be mushy or mealy. If you are buying for later, choose pears that are firm near the stem. To speed up the ripening of hard pears, place them in a paper sack with a whole banana and punch a few air holes in the sack. The pears should ripen in two to three days. You will know they are ripe when you begin to smell their heady sweet fragrance and the stem area starts to soften.

# blood orange *and* black grape ambrosia *with* cardamom hill maraschino cherries

BACK HOME IN INDIA, fruit salads are a part of everyday meals: plain fresh fruit medleys, fruit drizzled with honey, fruit seasoned with chiles and salt, or fruits in gingered custard. Ambrosia fruit salad reminds me of the fruit dessert recipes from my youth. There seems to be some disagreement over whether ambrosia is a salad or a dessert. After living in Atlanta for some years, I have come to the conclusion that it is served however the maker wishes it to be served. In other words, if you are doing the preparation and assembling, the course option is yours. On the other hand, if someone else is contributing the dish to the buffet, allow him or her to determine where it is placed. In this recipe, the addition of miniature marshmallows screams dessert, so that's what I'm going with—but you might want to also save a place for a Jell-O mold with marshmallows on the other end of the buffet, just in case.

1/2 cup heavy cream, cold

3 tablespoons white granulated sugar

1 cup (8 ounces) sour cream, cold

2 tablespoons (1 ounce) ginger liqueur or ginger brandy (see notes)

Zest of 1 lemon

3 cups (15 ounces) miniature marshmallows

4 blood oranges, peeled and segmented (see notes)

1 cup seedless black grapes, cut into halves

1/3 medium fresh pineapple, cored, trimmed, and cubed or frozen pineapple, thawed (1 cup)

1 cup sweetened frozen flaked coconut

1/2 cup (4 ounces) maraschino cherries, drained

**MAKES 6 SERVINGS**

Place the cream and sugar in the bowl of an electric mixer and, using the whisk attachment, whip the mixture until stiff peaks are formed, about 2 minutes. Add the sour cream and whisk to combine for 30 seconds; fold in the ginger liqueur and lemon zest. Remove attachment and add the marshmallows, blood oranges, black grapes, pineapple, coconut, and cherries and, with a large spatula, gently fold to combine. Transfer the salad to a glass serving bowl, place in the refrigerator, cover, and chill for an hour before serving.

# CARDAMOM HILL MARASCHINO CHERRIES

IT'S VERY HARD TO GO BACK to the oddly red "kiddie" maraschino cherries once you make your own at home. Plus, after making your cherries, you will have enough maraschino liqueur on hand to whip up classic cocktails such as the Southern Bride, the Hemingway Daiquiri, and the Beachcomber.

1 cup maraschino liqueur (I like to use Luxardo, Maraska, or Lazzaroni)

2 cups (1 pint) fresh sweet or sour cherries, stemmed and pitted

½ teaspoon green cardamom powder

Place the maraschino liqueur, cherries, and cardamom in a saucepan on medium heat and bring to a boil. Remove from heat and let the cherries cool in the liqueur. When cool, store in an airtight container. This makes 2 cups and keeps for weeks in the fridge.

**NOTES:** *There are several brands of ginger liqueur I very much enjoy, among them Domaine de Canton. DeKuyper also now makes both a ginger liqueur and a ginger-flavored brandy. Alternately, you can make your own by steeping ¼ cup candied ginger in 1½ cups brandy overnight.*

*To section oranges, slice a small section off the top and bottom of the fruit. Stand the fruit on a flat end on a cutting board. With a sharp thin knife, cut away the peel and the white pith, working in strips from top to bottom following the shape of the fruit. Working over a bowl, slice alongside the membrane of a section to the center of the fruit, releasing one side of the segment. Adjust the knife blade to face out from the exposed pulp. Cut along the membrane to free the citrus segment. Follow with the remaining segments. Use the juice in a recipe or sip it up yourself. The cook always deserves a special treat!*

# broiled grapefruit *and* **oranges** *with* **black pepper brandy sauce**

THE SUMMER CLIMATES OF BOTH OF MY SOUTHERN HOMELANDS are quite similar. During Atlanta winters, I don't mind heating up the kitchen until a light condensation cozily ripples the windowpanes, but the summertime is an entirely different story. The same holds true in Kerala. No one wants to fire up a hot stove when the temperature is insufferable. This recipe was created with the outside temperature in mind; it doesn't require baking, so it's quick and easy in the warm months, while the brandy and spices are heady and warming in the cooler months. It's an absolutely divine ending to a meal, whether served on a sunset-shadowed patio or on an incandescent table near the hearth. Serve this with a grapefruit spoon to enjoy every single bite of this aromatic citrus dessert. Cardamom Hill Maraschino Cherries (page 223) makes a nice garnish for the center of the grapefruits—if you want to get a little mid-twentieth-century *Mad Men*-esque with your presentation. To make a much-appreciated and welcomed gift for a host or hostess, handwrite this recipe on a card and attach it to a box of seasonal fresh grapefruit and oranges, bundled with a bottle of brandy.

3 ruby red grapefruits, halved around the equator

3 large navel oranges, halved around the equator

3 tablespoons dark-brown sugar, loosely packed

1/2 cup Black Pepper Brandy Sauce

Set oven to broil and heat with the rack 6 inches below the heat. Line a rimmed baking sheet pan with foil.

Place the grapefruit and orange halves, cut-side up, on the sheet pan. Using a sharp paring knife, cut just between the rind and the flesh all the way around of each fruit; this will allow the sugar to seep into the edges. On each fruit half, spread 1½ teaspoons of the brown sugar over the top of the exposed flesh but not the white pith or rind.

Place the fruits under the broiler and broil until the brown sugar is bubbly and beginning to darken and caramelize, about 3 to 5 minutes. Remove from the oven. Let cool for a minute. Place one grapefruit half and one orange half in each individual serving dish.

Give the brandy sauce a stir and pour over the broiled citrus. Serve warm.

## BLACK PEPPER BRANDY SAUCE

2 tablespoons unsalted butter

1/2 cup packed dark-brown sugar

1 teaspoon fresh coarsely ground black peppercorns

1/2 teaspoon kosher salt

1/2 cup (8 ounces) brandy

1 teaspoon pure vanilla extract

In a small saucepan over medium heat, heat the butter, sugar, black pepper, salt, and ¾ cup of water; stir and cook for 5 minutes. Add the brandy and vanilla extract. To avoid a flame-up, if using a gas stove, turn off the burner; if using an electric stove, reduce heat to low and stand back while adding the brandy and vanilla extract. Heat an additional minute. Set mixture aside while preparing the grapefruit and oranges.

**NOTES:** *For a nonalcoholic version, substitute a strongly brewed black tea, such as Earl Grey, flavored with bergamot and orange, for the brandy in this dessert recipe.*

# honeydew bavarian dusted
## *with* sugared black pepper

I CONFESS: THIS WAS A TOTAL FLUKE OF A RECIPE WHIPPED UP IN AN EMERGENCY. As cooks, we are often most creative when unexpectedly faced with having to make something with only the ingredients at hand. This recipe proves that, with a little thought, an amazing dish can be created almost out of thin air. Surprisingly, my on-hand ingredients turned into a delicious, palate-refreshing dessert.

This chilled dessert, with its absinthe-green hue, honey-fresh fruit flavor, and sour-cream tang, is elegant simplicity. Present this dessert with Sugared Black Pepper strewn over the top, and you will elevate the sense of pleasure and excitement for your guests.

1/2 cup passion fruit juice or unsweetened pineapple juice

3 envelopes unflavored gelatin

1 medium fresh honeydew melon (6 cups), rind removed and the flesh seeded and cubed (see notes)

3/4 cup white granulated sugar

1 cup (8 ounces) sour cream

Sugared Black Pepper, for garnish

In a small heavy saucepan, add the passion fruit juice and sprinkle the gelatin over it. Let the gelatin and juice sit until it softens, about 2 minutes. Place the pan over low heat, stirring constantly until the gelatin is dissolved, about 1 minute. Remove the pan from the heat and cool the mixture to room temperature.

In a food processor or blender, purée the melon and sugar until smooth. Transfer the melon mixture to a medium bowl, and stir in the gelatin and juice mixture. Whisk the sour cream to lighten it, then whisk it into the melon purée.

Spoon the melon mixture into a serving bowl or individual serving dishes. Chill in the refrigerator for at least 4 hours before serving. Garnish with Sugared Black Pepper right before serving.

**NOTES:** *The honeydew's sweet flesh turns from green to white as it ripens and is one of the few fruits that will continue to ripen once picked. Look for a creamy yellow melon with a waxy, but not shiny or fuzzy, skin with no blemishes and that feels heavy for its size. The vine end should be slightly soft and emit a fragrant, sweet smell when tested. Try to choose the ripest, sweetest melon for this dessert.*

*Although watermelon is too watery for this recipe, any variety of firm muskmelon, such as cantaloupe or casaba, is easily substituted for honeydew.*

## SUGARED BLACK PEPPER

1 tablespoon fresh coarsely ground black peppercorns

1 tablespoon white granulated sugar

In a small pan over high heat, mix the pepper and sugar together and stir constantly until it forms a granulated mixture of the black pepper and sugar, about 1 minute. Set aside to cool. Once the dessert has set and is ready to serve, sprinkle the black pepper mixture on top as a garnish. Do not sprinkle the Sugared Black Pepper on the Bavarians until right before serving. You want the mixture to stay crispy to offer a nice contrast to the palate.

# proper pepper pralines

DOWN IN NEW ORLEANS lives a lovely "confection-ess" by the name of Eva Louise Perry, known as Tee-Eva. In Louisiana the honorific *tee* is a shortened version of *taunte* (aunt) or *p'tit* (small, petite), both of which fit Tee-Eva to, well, a T. Keralans have a similar honorific, referring to dear female family friends and elders by their given names preceded by "aunty." Like some of my family friends and relatives, Tee-Eva has that joie de vivre I hope to possess when I'm well into my golden years. Tee-Eva learned to cook, as did I, from a long line of family members, and similarly, she developed a strong sweet tooth early in her childhood. Today, her shop, Tee-Eva's Old Fashioned Pies and Pralines, is consistently chosen by most New Orleanians as the place with the best praline. In fact, Tee-Eva is unofficially recognized as "the Praline Queen of the Big Easy." Pralines are an iconic confection in the Deep South, and these spiced buttermilk and orange pralines are dedicated to this bright, beaming woman. All over the world, other tees and aunties set an example for us to live life to its fullest, greeting each day with excitement and marveling at its unique wonders. You can visit Tee-Eva Perry on the corner of Dufossat and Magazine Streets next time you are in the Crescent City. Her granddaughter has taken over the day-to-day operations, but Tee-Eva can occasionally be found cooking and, at times, covering the late shift. In the store you will find her authentic New Orleans snowballs. They come in a variety of flavors and can be topped with crumbled pralines and other deliciously sweet adornments. Try breaking up these pepper pralines and stirring them into your favorite sorbet or sherbet.

Trust me on this: use a candy thermometer when making this recipe. I know there are drop-in-water tests or protestations of "Grandmama didn't use one," but since we all can't be like Tee-Eva, who after a lifetime of making pralines has the method down pat, just use a thermometer and cast your worries aside.

2 tablespoons unsalted butter

1 cup buttermilk

2 tablespoon light corn syrup

1½ cups white granulated sugar

1½ cups packed light-brown sugar

Zest of 2 oranges

2 teaspoons fresh coarsely ground black peppercorns

½ teaspoon kosher salt

1½ cups (24 ounces) chopped pecans

Line a large sheet pan with parchment paper. In a heavy 2-quart saucepan over medium-low heat, add the butter, buttermilk, corn syrup, sugar, brown sugar, orange zest, black pepper, and salt. Stir the mixture constantly with a wooden spoon until the sugars have dissolved, the mixture comes to a boil, and a candy thermometer reads 235°F, about 8 minutes. Quickly fold in the pecans and continue cooking, constantly stirring for another minute, then remove from heat and allow the mixture to cool for 5 minutes. After 5 minutes, beat the mixture with a wooden spoon just until it begins to thicken and the glossy sheen turns creamy, about 2 to 3 minutes.

Drop heaping tablespoons onto the lined sheet tray and let cool for 30 minutes.

Pecans can be bought in the baking or produce sections of any grocery store. However the freshest, best pecans at the best prices are usually found at farmers' markets between September and December. Try to buy from some of the smaller purveyors for maximum freshness. Sellers like these sell only what is produced locally, often in limited quantities, since they only sell seasonally, and once the year's crop is gone, you will have to look elsewhere. Good, fresh pecans will make a difference in the taste of your recipes. They are best kept refrigerated when purchased for immediate use or can be frozen for use later. Freezing does not diminish the flavor of pecans at all.

# lemon yogurt cake *with* coconut lemon ginger glaze

Yogurt and coconut are always available in my kitchens. Consequently, this is a cake I make time and time again. The glaze, made with grated coconut and ginger, soaks down deep into tunnels poked into the cake with a wooden skewer, which keeps this cake incredibly moist for days.

MAKES ONE 9-INCH BUNDT CAKE, 12 TO 16 SERVINGS

1½ pounds butter (6 sticks) unsalted butter plus 2 tablespoons for greasing cake pan, at room temperature

2½ cups unbleached all-purpose flour plus more for dusting

2½ cups white granulated sugar

2 tablespoons fresh lemon zest

¼ cup freshly squeezed lemon juice

6 large whole eggs

1 cup (8 ounces) plain Greek-style yogurt

1 teaspoon kosher salt

½ teaspoon baking soda

½ teaspoon baking powder

Heat the oven to 350°F. Grease and flour a 9-inch Bundt cake pan; chill in the refrigerator.

In an electric mixer bowl fitted with a paddle attachment, beat the granulated sugar and lemon zest at low speed for 1 minute to flavor the sugar. Add the butter, and beat the mixture together at medium speed until fluffy, about 3 minutes. Add ¼ cup lemon juice; beat until blended. Add the eggs, one at a time, beating for about 3 minutes. Add the yogurt to the mixture, and beat for another 2 minutes.

In a medium bowl, whisk together the flour, salt, baking soda, and baking powder and add to the flour mixture; beat for another 3 minutes, until everything is incorporated and the batter is thick.

Pour the batter into the prepared pan and bake for 55 minutes to 1 hour, or until a long wooden skewer inserted in the center comes out clean. Cool cake in the pan on a cooling rack for 1 hour. Turn the cake onto a plate, and let it cool again. (Meanwhile, make the glaze.) Prick a few holes in the cake with the skewer, and pour the coconut ginger glaze over the cake.

# COCONUT LEMON GINGER GLAZE

Guardian Angel Food Cake (page 242) is glorious topped with this glaze, too.

2 cups powdered confectioners' sugar, sifted

2 tablespoons cornstarch

4 teaspoons peeled, grated fresh ginger

1/2 teaspoon kosher salt

Zest of 2 lemons

1/4 cup freshly squeezed lemon juice

1 cup frozen, grated fresh coconut, thawed

1 1/2 cups coconut milk

In a medium saucepan, mix the sugar, cornstarch, grated ginger, salt, lemon zest and juice, grated coconut, and coconut milk. Cook over medium heat, stirring until thickened, for about 15 minutes.

# mango sweet sticky rice

AS I NOTED EARLIER, mangoes and recipes using them comprise my favorite foods. In fact, the very earliest memories I have of food revolve around mangoes and mango season. My great-aunt Rita Netto stored straw-lined baskets full of mangoes of all varieties in a darkened room off her kitchen behind cobalt blue doors. Even as a very small child, I adored the mangoes' spectrum of colors: bright red, radiant yellow, pinkish orange, deep purple, and delicate soft green. Later, as a schoolgirl, I would rush home from school to simply stand in that room. Eating fresh mango, I imagined the succulent flesh must taste just like sweet sunshine. It is that same sense of delight and discovery of simple yet potent ingredients that inspires me today. As a result, I consider myself an expert and purist when it comes to mangoes.

Jasmine rice is grown primarily in Thailand, Laos, Cambodia, and Vietnam. It is a long-grain rice possessing a heady aroma, soft texture, and slightly sweet flavor. It adds a wonderfully aromatic quality that seems to get along well with the mangoes, while the black sesame seeds punctuate it with a bold look and nutty flavor.

2 cups jasmine rice

1 teaspoon kosher salt

1½ cups coconut milk

¼ cup white granulated sugar

3 medium (3 cups) ripe mangoes, peeled, pitted, and cut into ½-inch cubes

3 tablespoons cane syrup or 3 to 4 tablespoons honey

1 teaspoon freshly grated nutmeg

1 teaspoon black sesame seeds (see notes)

In a 3-quart pot add the rice, 4 cups water, and salt and bring to a boil over high heat. Stir, turn heat to low, tightly cover, and cook until the liquid is absorbed, about 12 minutes, making sure to not remove lid. Turn off the heat; keep the lid on and let it sit for another 10 minutes, then lift the lid and use a fork to fluff the rice.

In a separate bowl, whisk the coconut milk and sugar together and pour over and fold into the rice. Let the rice cool to room temperature and attain the consistency of a firm rice pudding.

Scoop about 1 cup of the rice into an individual serving bowl, spoon about ½ cup of the mangoes into each bowl of rice, drizzle ½ teaspoon of the cane syrup or ½ tablespoon of the honey over the rice and mangoes, then dust with the freshly grated nutmeg and garnish with the black sesame seeds.

**NOTES:** *Black sesame seeds are a variety of sesame seed with the hulls still covering the ecru seed. I think the black hull-on seeds have a stronger, nuttier flavor—plus I love the way they look. Black sesame seeds are often found in specialty baking stores and sushi supply shops.*

## VALLIAMMI, MANGOES, AND MEMORIES

My great-aunt Rita Netto lived to be ninety-one years old and passed away when I was a young teen. I called her Valliammi, which means "big mother." Although she was not big in stature, her heart was all encompassing. She was frail, beautiful, and pale skinned with light gray eyes. She never married. All of us grandchildren were her babies. It was her home that I loved to go to the most in the summertime; it was the house where all the mangoes were stored to ripen in the room behind the vibrant blue doors . . . oh, how I loved that room, seemingly secreted behind those doors, hiding all those baskets of lovely mangoes along with colorful stalks of bananas hanging from the ceiling, with hay scattered all over the floor. It was my special place. Behind her house was a huge tree that bore fresh, sweet tamarind. I whiled away many an afternoon in its shade, eating ripe sweet tamarind with my friends, watching the banana plants, papaya trees, and coconut palms swaying in the wind. Valliammi's home was a magical place. When I was thirteen years old, she was diagnosed with dementia, and I became her caregiver. I fed her hot tea and warm rolls dipped in the tea every morning before I went to school. I came running home on a break from school only to turn around and rush one house over to see her and have afternoon tea. Toward the end of her life, I had the privilege of bathing her and combing her hair every day. She was a very special woman in my life. I was by her bed-side when she took her last breath, peacefully and surrounded by love.

# orange blossom vermicelli kheer

THIS SIMPLE, DECADENT DESSERT is made with bits of broken wheat pasta. Having been around for generations, *kheer* remains a comforting traditional dish in every Indian household, especially for birthdays, religious holidays, and celebrations. Versions of *kheer* can be found all across India: in the north it is often made with cow's milk, and in the west cooks sometimes use buffalo milk. In Kerala, this pudding is most often made with coconut milk. Here in Atlanta, I've found that a sweetened condensed milk version is wildly popular. So borrowing from both my southern regions, I've incorporated the sweet floral notes along with my spice favorites, cardamom and nutmeg, into the condensed milk to produce a "my two Souths" version of *kheer*. This recipe produces an elegant, toasted noodle cream, perfumed with orange flower water.

1 tablespoon ghee

8 ounces vermicelli, uncooked and broken into 1/2-inch pieces (see notes)

1 quart (4 cups) whole milk

3/4 cup (6 ounces) sweetened condensed milk

1 tablespoon orange flower water (see notes)

1 teaspoon green cardamom powder

1/4 teaspoon nutmeg powder

3 tablespoons roughly chopped, raw, shelled pistachios

In a heavy-bottomed medium saucepan over medium high, melt the ghee. Add the vermicelli. Toast the pasta, stirring continuously to turn all the strands, until golden brown, about 2 minutes. Remove the pasta from the heat and pour the toasted vermicelli on a small plate and set aside.

In the same pan over medium-low heat, add the milk, sweetened condensed milk, and orange flower water. Stir the cardamom and nutmeg into the milk mixture. Heat the mixture over medium heat, taking care not to scorch the milk, just until the mixture begins to consistently foam across the surface.

Add the roasted vermicelli and cook over medium heat, stirring constantly, until the pasta turns soft, about 5 minutes. Remove from heat.

The *kheer* should have a pudding-like consistency. Spoon into individual serving dishes or a single large bowl and garnish with pistachios. While I love this dessert served warm, it's equally delicious at room temperature or chilled.

**NOTES:** *Because of the popularity of kheer, many specialty markets now offer a preroasted version of vermicelli. Look for brand names like Bambino, MTR, or Anakali. To use these products, simply skip the roasting stage of this recipe.*

*When breaking up the vermicelli to make kheer, the pieces tend to shoot out all over the kitchen, ricocheting off every surface. ("Don't shoot your eye out, kid!") The bag from a loaf of sandwich bread works particularly well to keep the little projectiles corralled. Slip the pasta into the bag and hit it with a rolling pin, or bang it against the counter, to break the pasta up into small pieces.*

*Orange flower water is a clear, perfumed by-product of the distillation of fresh bitter orange flower blossoms. Contrary to what one might think, it does not taste like oranges. Instead, it adds a fragrant floral aspect to dishes. It is a common ingredient in many Mexican and Spanish dessert recipes, where it is called* agua de azahar, *so a local* tienda *is likely a good purchasing source. If you are fond of floral notes, try substituting 2 teaspoons of rosewater for the orange flower water in this recipe for a pleasing variation.*

# cinnamon biscuit bramble cobbler *and* cream

I LOVE BLACKBERRIES, BISCUITS, and cream! Once a good bit of cinnamon gets in the mix, well, I am simply a goner. This jammy biscuit-topped cobbler served warm with a pour of sweet cream has me running my finger around the bowl to make sure I get every drop of the violet fruit cream. Perhaps it's another British holdover to call blackberries brambles. I like the way the word *bramble* makes me think of a nice summer ramble.

## DOUGH

8 tablespoons (1 stick) unsalted butter, chilled and cut into small pieces, plus 2 tablespoons, softened, for greasing casserole

1½ cups unbleached all-purpose flour

2/3 cup fine granulated raw sugar, divided

3 teaspoons baking powder

¼ teaspoon kosher salt

¾ teaspoon cinnamon powder

1 cup heavy whipping cream plus an additional ¼ cup cream for serving, if desired

1 large egg, beaten

## BLACKBERRIES

¾ cup fine granulated raw sugar

2 tablespoons cornstarch

¼ teaspoon cinnamon powder

6 cups fresh or frozen blackberries (see notes)

Zest and juice of 1 lime

1 tablespoon amaretto

**MAKES 6 TO 8 SERVINGS**

Heat the oven to 400°F. Grease a 2-quart casserole dish.

In a large bowl combine the flour, ⅓ cup of the sugar, baking powder, salt, and cinnamon. Cut the butter into the flour mixture using fingertips or a pastry blender until the butter is incorporated and the mixture is slightly lumpy and loose.

Add the cream and beaten egg. Using a fork, blend the dough until it is well mixed. Set aside the dough and prepare the blackberries.

Place ½ cup of water in a medium saucepan over medium heat, and add the sugar, cornstarch, and cinnamon powder. Slowly whisk until the mixture begins to simmer. Add the blackberries, lime zest and juice, and amaretto. Cook and gently stir with a spoon for 5 minutes, or until the berries are tender and glossy and the filling begins to look like a thick jam.

Pour the blackberry filling into the prepared dish. Spoon heaping tablespoons of the dough over the filling. Sprinkle the remaining ⅓ cup of sugar over the cobbler.

Bake for 25 to 30 minutes, or until the top is deeply browned and the blackberries are bubbling. Set the cobbler on a cooling rack to cool for at least 25 minutes. Serve with a few tablespoons of cream poured over each individual serving.

**NOTES:** *Blackberries are at their peak from June through September around the southern US. Look for berries without any hulls attached. A ripe berry will lose its hull when picked. Blackberries do not continue to ripen once picked so choose carefully for the sweetest flavor.*

*Try blueberries or plums in this cinnamon-scented cobbler swimming in sweet cream.*

# guardian angel food cake

MY FIRST NAME, ASHA, means "hope" in Malayalam, the official language of Kerala. My middle name is Goretti. I was named for Saint Maria Goretti, the patron saint of young women, purity, and chastity. I was taught at a very young age that she was my guardian angel and would stay with me throughout my life and would accompany me into heaven. She is often depicted holding white lilies and a knife. I like that image as it shows she is a strong-willed woman. She is also the patron saint of forgiveness, one of the most freeing personal acts.

When I make this lofty, white cake, I like to think of loved ones who have passed and the idea of angels. While sifting the flour, sugar, and spices together six times, there is plenty of time for reflection. Watching the whip transform the egg whites to a cloud-like meringue seems a bit miraculous every time.

Glaze this heavenly cake with Coconut Ginger Glaze (page 233) or top slices with Cardamom Hill Maraschino Cherries (page 223) or Tarragon-Laced Apricot Compote (page 216). This cake can also be used as the base for Colonial Trifle (page 244).

14 tablespoons unbleached all-purpose flour

1/4 teaspoon finely ground white peppercorns

1/8 teaspoon freshly grated nutmeg

1/2 cup confectioners' sugar

1 1/2 cups egg whites (about large 12 eggs), at room temperature

1 teaspoon cream of tartar (see notes)

1/2 teaspoon fine sea salt

1 teaspoon pure vanilla extract

1/4 teaspoon pure almond extract

1 cup superfine white granulated sugar (see notes page 149)

**MAKES ONE 10-INCH CAKE, 10 SERVINGS**

Heat the oven to 350°F. Place baking rack on the next to the bottom rung with plenty of room for the 10-inch cake pan to fit. Sift the flour, white pepper, nutmeg, and confectioners' sugar together six times.

Place the egg whites in the large bowl of an electric mixer with a whisk attachment. Whip the eggs on medium speed until opaque and frothy. Add the cream of tartar and salt; increase the speed and whip on high, until the egg whites are fluffy. Add 1 tablespoon of water and the vanilla and almond extracts. Slowly add the superfine sugar, 1 tablespoonful at a time, whipping on high until the mixture is very thick and airy.

Using a very large spatula, working in three additions, fold the flour into the meringue; carefully, yet thoroughly, incorporate the flour until the batter is mostly streak free. Scrape the batter into a 10-inch angel food cake pan and spread evenly.

Bake the cake for 45 minutes, or until the top is browned and the cake springs back when lightly touched. Remove the cake from the oven and invert to cool for at least 1 hour. When the cake is cool, turn right side up and run a very sharp knife around both the outer and inner edges of the cake. Invert the pan and gently press the cake from the pan onto a platter.

**NOTES:** *If your pan does not have tabs or feet or a raised center tube that will keep air circulating around the cake as it cools bottom side up, place the inverted cake on an inverted ramekin or slide the center tube over a short bottle. Air must flow around the cake so it does not get steamy and collapse. Cooling upside down helps the cake retain its height.*

*Cream of tartar is a fine white powder produced as a by-product of wine making. The acidic white powder helps to stabilize egg whites while making meringue and gives them extra volume. It also helps keep the meringue from weeping.*

Cold eggs will separate much easier than room-temperature eggs. Separate eggs right out of the refrigerator, then allow the egg whites to come to room temp before whipping to the highest volume. Be sure you do not leave one speck of egg yolk, or fingerprint of an egg yolk, in the whites or on the bowl, whip, or spatula. Any fat will keep the egg whites from whipping up nicely. Also, do not whack the whip on the side of the bowl to dislodge meringue that is clinging to the whip. Doing this will knock the air out of the whites. Instead, tap the whip against your fist to dislodge the meringue.

# colonial trifle

IN MY FAMILY, we have women with very familiar Portuguese and British first names. These two countries made huge impacts on Indian culture, extending beyond religion and cooking to include the naming of one's children. Yes, the Portuguese and British who colonized India brought into my family names like Hazel, Carmel, and Margaret. So, in keeping with her queenly name, my aunt Victoria embraced the English dessert called trifle and made it her own. It was her specialty, and she served it at every family gathering.

If you make your own angel food cake (page 242) for the trifle, like Aunt Victoria would have done, you'll get terrific results. But I am a working mother and a realist, so if I don't have the time to bake a cake, I'm happy as can be grabbing one from the grocery store bakery section. It does not give me even the slightest pang of guilt. And, frankly, once the fluffy white cake gets the mango treatment, no one will ever know you cut a tiny corner by purchasing the cake.

**MAKES 8 SERVINGS**

1 store-bought angel food cake (7-inches round) or Guardian Angel Food Cake (page 242), cut into about 20 slices

1/3 cup (2.5 ounces) mango preserves (see notes)

2 navel oranges, peeled and sectioned

6 to 8 medium fresh strawberries (1 cup), hulled and sliced

1 medium fresh mango, peeled, stoned, and cubed or frozen mango, thawed (1 cup)

1/3 fresh pineapple, peeled, cored, and cubed or frozen pineapple, thawed (1 cup)

3 cups (24 ounces) Mango Curd

1 cup heavy whipping cream

1 teaspoon sherry

2 tablespoons confectioners' sugar

1/4 cup (2 ounces) candied pecans

Spread the mango preserves over one side of each slice of angel food cake. Arrange half of the cake pieces, preserves sides down, in the bottom of a 3-quart trifle bowl or other clear glass bowl. Arrange half of the fruit over the cake. Spoon half of the Mango Curd over the fruit in the bowl. Repeat with remaining cake, fruit, and Mango Curd.

Whip the cream with the sherry and confectioners' sugar until stiff peaks are formed. Top the trifle with the whipped cream.

Refrigerate the trifle for 8 to 12 hours. Garnish with candied pecans.

## MANGO CURD

1 cup Greek-style yogurt

3/4 cup mango purée

4 tablespoons white granulated sugar

In a medium bowl, whisk the Greek yogurt and add the mango purée and sugar to make the mango curd.

**NOTES:** *If you cannot find mango preserves in the market, make a recipe of Fiery Mango Jam (page 51) and omit the peppers.*

## CANDIED PECANS

1/2 cup white granulated sugar

1/2 teaspoon kosher salt

1 egg white

1/4 pound pecan halves

Heat the oven to 275°F. In a small bowl, whisk the sugar, salt, egg white, and 1 tablespoon of water until frothy. Toss the pecans in the egg-white mixture with a fork until the pecans are coated evenly. Spread the pecans onto a baking sheet. Bake, stirring once after 15 minutes, until the pecans are glazed, about 30 minutes. (Keep a close watch so these nuts do not burn.) Allow the pecans to cool completely before topping the trifle.

# smoky hazelnut chocolate cookies

I HAVE NO DOUBT THAT, IF I ALLOWED HIM TO DO SO, Ethan would eat a jar of Nutella in one sitting. To ensure that this creamy hazelnut spread wound up as an ingredient rather than the main course, I realized I had to come up with a Nutella recipe for my boy. Given his well-practiced sweet tooth, a cookie was the obvious and easy direction to take. But, as you may have gathered, my son is his mother's boy: Ethan loves spice in every form and shape as I do. When I added a hint of sugared, smoked paprika to Nutella cookie dough, I knew I had hit it out of the park. These are now Ethan's favorite cookies, and he won't even give them time to cool before snatching them up. I think my kid has a rather grown-up sense of taste for a ten-year-old. I wonder where he got it? My favorite part of this recipe is mixing the dough with my hands, and Ethan loves to roll up his sleeves and get in on the action.

1 cup unbleached all-purpose flour

1/2 cup white granulated sugar

2 teaspoons smoked sweet paprika, divided

2 large eggs

1 cup (8 ounces) Nutella, at room temperature

1/4 cup (2 ounces) hazelnuts, roasted, skinned, and chopped (see notes)

Cooking spray

1 tablespoon confectioners' sugar, for dusting

Heat the oven to 350°F.

In a medium bowl, using your hands, mix together the flour, sugar, 1½ teaspoons of the smoked paprika, and eggs to form a crumbly dough. Mix in the Nutella and hazelnuts and work to form a smooth dough, no more than 2 minutes.

Spray a cookie sheet with cooking spray and set aside.

Separate the dough into 10 equal parts, using your palms to roll them into round balls. Place the balls on the cookie sheet, 1 inch apart. Bake for 6 to 8 minutes, or until the cookies are flat discs, crisp around the edges. Remove the cookies from the oven; dust with the remaining smoked paprika and confectioners' sugar. Eat them immediately—like Ethan—or after they have cooled down.

**NOTES:** *To roast and skin hazelnuts, toast the nuts on a sheet pan in a 350°F oven for 12 to 15 minutes or until they are beginning to brown and are very fragrant. Place the nuts in a kitchen towel and gather up the edges to form a bundle. Rub the nuts together in the towel to remove most of the dark-brown skin.*

# amma's toffee christmas cake

WE NEVER REALLY BAKED THAT OFTEN AT HOME in coastal southern India. At Carmel Compound, baking was reserved for special occasions that mainly revolved around Christian holidays, especially Christmas. I grew up in a Roman Catholic home, and as is the custom in Kerala, our preparations for Christmas celebrations began the first week of December. In Kerala, families and churches alike would competitively re-create miniature Nativity scenes, which visiting carolers later judged. The winners were announced and given gifts at Midnight Mass on Christmas Eve. It should be noted that Christians are not the only celebrants of late-year holidays in India. December in Kerala is a happy time for people of all castes, colors, and creeds; it's a time when family members scattered abroad return home to engage in a gleeful celebration of family and humanity. In our home, as the decorating commenced, so did the preparation of dried fruit for holiday goodies. Rum was bought to soak and plump prunes and raisins—all destined for inclusion in Amma's impressive Christmas cake. Since the children of Kerala are the focus of Christmas festivities, I retain vivid memories of my childhood Christmases: cakes being assembled while Elvis Presley, Bing Crosby, and Jim Reeves sang carols on the stereo, as the temperature hovered around 80 degrees. Sounds exotic, right? Well, suffice it to say, Christmas in Kerala is a lot like Christmas in Atlanta—just with fewer ice storm warnings.

My grandmother's almost-black, rum-soaked toffee cake recipe, re-created below, is full of raisins, prunes, and candied orange. She made literally dozens of these cakes during the holidays, packing them in tins for voyages to family and friends in the neighborhood and around the world.

1 cup chopped pitted prunes

1 cup (8 ounces) dark seedless raisins

½ cup (4 ounces) golden seedless raisins or sultanas

3 to 5 dried figs (¼ cup), stemmed and rinsed

¼ cup (2 ounces) candied orange peel

½ cup (4 ounces) port wine

½ cup (4 ounces) plus 3 tablespoons dark rum

8 tablespoons (1 stick) unsalted butter plus more for greasing cake pan, softened

1 cup unbleached all-purpose flour, sifted, plus more for dusting

1 cup packed dark-brown sugar

5 large eggs

1½ teaspoons baking powder

½ teaspoon allspice powder

½ teaspoon cinnamon powder

¼ teaspoon clove powder

¼ teaspoon freshly grated nutmeg

¼ teaspoon kosher salt

2 teaspoons unsulphured molasses

Place the dried fruits, port, and rum into a food processor. Pulse the mixture until the dried fruit is broken down into smaller chunks. Remove mixture from food processor to a lidded container, and let the fruits marinate for at least 48 hours.

When ready to bake the cake, heat the oven to 350°F.

Grease a 9-inch round cake pan. Line the bottom with parchment paper, and grease the paper and side of the pan. Dust the paper and side with flour, tapping out any excess.

With an electric mixer, whip the butter and brown sugar for 2 minutes, then add the eggs one at a time and mix at low speed until very well incorporated, about another 2 minutes. In a medium bowl, whisk the flour, baking powder, allspice, cinnamon, clove, nutmeg, and salt together, combining well. Add the flour mixture ½ cup at a time to the butter and sugar mixture, and beat at medium for another 2 minutes. Add the molasses and whip for another 30 seconds. Add the rum-soaked fruit to the mixer a little at a time, and mix to combine all the ingredients, about another 2 minutes.

Pour the batter into the prepared cake pan.

Fill a large roasting pan halfway with water and place on the center rack of the oven. Set the cake pan in the water and bake for 1 hour 30 minutes, or until the cake is set like a thick pudding.

Allow cake to cool for 30 minutes, then remove from pan and drizzle with the remaining rum.

**NOTES:** *Baking the dense, fruit-packed rum cake in a water bath keeps it moist throughout, allowing the middle to set while protecting the sides from drying out.*

*Southern literature is another gift of my new home that I have grown to love. Each December, I re-read Truman Capote's charming tale of holiday baking and making of simple gifts as a boy in his 1963 short story "A Christmas Memory."*

# tangy lattice-top rhubarb pie

EVEN THOUGH THE BRITISH are keen on rhubarb recipes, they seemed to have overlooked sharing that secret ingredient while in southern India. I never even heard of rhubarb until I was in my twenties, and in those twenty years, boy, did I miss out on this deliciousness! Once I was introduced to rhubarb, I savored its strong, tart taste and was amazed at how well it paired with sugar and spice. And I adore a good pucker!

Some confusion still exists about whether it is a vegetable or a fruit: most places call it a vegetable, but in the US, it has been designated as a fruit since it is primarily used in sweet recipes. Eaten raw, the stalks are similar in texture to celery, and in some parts of the world, they are often dipped in sugar and eaten as treats, while other parts choose to dip them in salt or red pepper flakes. Obviously, rhubarb is the perfect ingredient for my love of sweet and sour desserts—and I take this recipe one step further with the addition of banana peppers. Serve this lattice-topped pie with vanilla frozen yogurt.

2 pounds rhubarb (about 15 stalks), trimmed, cut into 3-inch-thick pieces, or 48 ounces chopped frozen rhubarb (about 6 cups) (see notes)

1½ cups plus 2 teaspoons white granulated sugar

1 teaspoon green cardamom powder

1 teaspoon freshly grated orange zest

6 fresh banana peppers, seeded and thinly sliced

¼ cup (2 ounces) orange marmalade

¼ cup (2 ounces) cornstarch

½ teaspoon kosher salt

1 Cream Cheese Piecrust (page 39)

1 large egg, lightly beaten

1 tablespoon heavy whipping cream

**MAKES ONE 9-INCH PIE, 8 SERVINGS**

In a medium bowl, mix the rhubarb, 1½ cups of the granulated sugar, cardamom, orange zest, banana peppers, marmalade, cornstarch, and salt.

Dust a rolling pin and work surface lightly with flour. Divide the dough in half and roll each half into a circle. Carefully place one dough circle into a 9-inch pie plate, and gently press into the plate. Trim excess dough around the edge with scissors.

Pour in the pie filling.

Cut the other dough circle into eleven ½-inch-wide strips. Arrange 6 dough strips on top of the filling, spacing evenly apart. Arrange 5 dough strips on top of the filling in the opposite direction, forming a lattice. Pinch the strip ends to the bottom crust edge and seal with fingers.

Refrigerate for 30 minutes.

Heat the oven to 375°F.

Combine the egg and cream, and using a pastry brush, paint the piecrust with the mixture. Sprinkle the top lattice crust with the remaining 2 teaspoons of sugar.

Bake for 1½ hours, or until the crust is deep golden brown and the filling is bubbly. Let the pie cool on a cooling rack for 1½ hours before serving.

**NOTES:** *Fresh rhubarb has red-tinged stalks with bright green leaves. The leaves are inedible, so don't make the mistake of using them. You'll likely find only the stalks in produce sections, but sometimes farmers sell them with the leaves attached. Rhubarb grown in hothouses is available between late January and April, while field varieties are in season May through July. Stalks should be firm, crisp, and turgid, not flaccid.*

*To trim tough or mature rhubarb stalks, cut a thin slice off each end of the stalk. Working at the top end of the stalk, cut almost through from the inside of the stalk toward the outer colored skin. Pull back the outer peel and discard. Repeat this process with the other side of the stalk.*

*I like to round up any of the dough scraps and brush them with remaining egg wash, sprinkle with a little sugar, and bake on a sheet pan in the oven along with the pie for 10 minutes. They make a delightful tea-time snack, or a treat for the cook while waiting for the pie to cool.*

# bittersweet bird's eye tart

I LOVE THE SMALL BIRD'S EYE CHILES FROM LOUISIANA, *piment zozo*. The *zozo* is an endearment for bird in French, *oiseau*. They are small and deep red with an ardent heat. When steeped in cream, the chiles pass along a tongue-tingling heat to this deeply dark chocolate tart. If you are fond of chocolate truffles, dust the top of the tart with cocoa powder for another level of chocolate experience.

Rolling the dough for the crust between the pieces of plastic eliminates the need for dusting the work surface with extra flour, which would toughen the crust. If the dough is too hard to roll right out of the freezer, give it 5 minutes to warm up, then whack it with a rolling pin to flatten the dough a bit and get the rolling process started.

## CRUST

8 tablespoons (1 stick) plus 1 tablespoon unsalted butter, cold

1/2 cup fine granulated raw sugar

3/4 teaspoon pure vanilla extract

1/4 teaspoon kosher sea salt

6 tablespoons (1½ ounces) Dutch-processed cocoa powder

1/2 teaspoon Kashmiri chili powder

3/4 cup unbleached all-purpose flour

In a food processor fitted with the blade attachment or bowl of an electric mixer, combine the butter, sugar, vanilla extract, and salt for 2 minutes, or until the mixture is creamy. Add the cocoa and chili powder; mix to make a dark paste. Add the flour all at once and pulse to make a crumbly dough. Form the dough into a large flat disc, wrap in plastic wrap, and refrigerate for 30 minutes for the dough to rest and chill. Roll the dough between two pieces of plastic wrap to keep it from sticking to the work surface and for ease in transferring the dough to the pan.

Roll the dough into a ⅛-inch-thick 11-inch round. Remove the top sheet of plastic wrap and use the bottom piece to help position the dough in a 10-inch fluted tart pan with a removable bottom. Press the dough into the bottom and up the sides of the pan. Trim any excess dough, and prick the bottom of the crust several times with the tines of a fork. Cover the crust and refrigerate the tart shell for at least 30 minutes or up to 2 days.

When ready to bake the tart shell, heat oven to 375°F. Bake the shell for 12 to 14 minutes or until the crust is crisp around the edges. Cool the crust in the pan on a cooling rack until completely cooled.

## FILLING

10 ounces bittersweet chocolate, chopped into small pieces

1¼ cups heavy cream

1 dried red bird's eye chile or Thai chile, seeded and chopped

Cocoa powder for garnish, if desired

Place the chocolate in a medium bowl and set aside. In a small saucepan over medium heat, warm the cream with the chile for 1 minute. Bring the cream to a simmer. Strain the cream over the chocolate. Do not stir. Let the mixture sit undisturbed for 30 seconds. Using a spatula, gently stir the chocolate until the mixture is smooth. Try to incorporate as little air as possible into the chocolate to make the smoothest possible filling. Pour the filling into the prepared crust. Tilt and gently shake and rotate the tart to evenly distribute the filling over the crust. Cover and refrigerate for 1 hour or up to 2 days. When ready to serve, allow the tart to come to room temperature and dust with cocoa powder, if desired.

To remove the tart from the two-piece pan, set the cooled tart on a can (I find sweetened condensed milk cans to be the perfect size) and press down evenly on the rim of the ring. It will slide onto the table. Lift the tart off the can and move to a serving plate.

**NOTES:** *Tilting the crust as opposed to spreading the filling creates a smoother surface on the finished tart. If I need to store or travel with this tart, I cover my tart with an inverted bowl or cake dome to keep the plastic from marring the surface of the shiny tart.*

# three spice carrot cake

I CAN THINK OF NO BETTER TRIBUTE TO MY MOTHER than sharing her favorite carrot cake recipe. And because my mother enjoyed using the best of her *masala dhabba*, or spice tin, this carrot cake surprises both your eyes and your taste buds. The cream cheese icing retains its ivory hue, but it's flecked with cracked black peppercorns. And while the consistency of the cake will be familiar, a closer look at the moist crumbs reveals tiny hints of cardamom and clove. Since my mother made this cake with care and love every single time, I consider the gift of her recipe a treasure. I am honored to offer it now as a gift to you.

**MAKES ONE 10-INCH ROUND LAYER CAKE, 16 SERVINGS**

2 tablespoons unsalted butter for greasing cake pans

3 1/2 cups unbleached all-purpose flour plus more for dusting

1 tablespoon baking powder

1 1/2 teaspoons baking soda (see notes)

1 tablespoon fresh coarsely ground black peppercorns

2 teaspoons clove powder

2 tablespoons green cardamom powder

2 cups white granulated sugar

9 large eggs

1 3/4 cups canola oil

6 carrots, peeled and grated (3 cups)

Heat the oven to 350°F degrees. Grease two 10-inch round cake pans. Line the bottoms with parchment paper, and grease the paper and sides of the pans. Dust the paper and sides with flour, tapping out any excess.

In a bowl, sift the flour, baking powder, and baking soda together, then mix in the pepper, clove, and cardamom. Set aside.

In an electric mixer on medium speed, whip the sugar and eggs until light and fluffy, about 3 minutes. With mixer running, add the oil slowly to maintain the emulsion.

Add the dry ingredients to the sugar, egg, and oil mixture, and mix on medium speed for another 3 minutes. Add the carrots and mix for another 2 minutes.

Pour the cake batter into the prepared pans, dividing evenly between the two. Bake for 45 minutes, or until golden brown and a wooden skewer inserted into the centers of the cakes comes out clean. Let the cake cool in the pans on a cooling rack for 15 minutes. Run a knife around the edge of the cakes to loosen, then turn them out onto a rack and let them cool completely. Make the frosting.

# CREAM CHEESE ICING

1¹/2 pounds (2 cups) cream cheese, at room temperature

16 tablespoons (2 sticks) unsalted butter

2¹/2 cups powdered confectioners' sugar, sifted

1 tablespoon fresh coarsely ground black peppercorns

1 tablespoon green cardamom powder

1 teaspoon clove powder

In an electric mixer with the paddle attachment, beat the cream cheese and butter at medium speed until creamy, about 3 to 5 minutes. Gradually add the confectioners' sugar, pepper, cardamom, and clove while beating at low speed until blended for another 3 to 4 minutes.

**FROST THE CAKES:** Using a serrated knife, trim the rounded tops of both cakes. (Gobble up all of the scraps!) Place one trimmed cake, cut-side up, on a serving platter. Spread 1¹/2 cups of the frosting over the cake. Top with second trimmed cake, cut-side down. Spread 1¹/2 cups frosting over cake. Spread the remaining cream cheese icing over the sides. Refrigerate the cake for 1 hour before serving.

**NOTES:** *Baking powder loses its freshness when exposed to humidity. Write the date on a newly opened can to help keep track of how old the powder is. To check for freshness, mix 2 teaspoons of baking powder in very hot water: it should fizz and pop right away. If it doesn't, discard the remainder and pick up a fresh can. Your baked goods will thank you, especially this cake, which needs a lot of oomph to raise the batter filled with carrots.*

*For checking if the cake is done, if I can't lay my hands on a wooden skewer, I'll use a piece of spaghetti to test for doneness.*

Some baking friends of mine taught me a few tricks for working with parchment paper while baking and decorating cakes. First, trace the bottom of the cake pan in the center of a piece of parchment paper at least 4 inches larger all around than the pan. Next, fold the paper in half lengthwise and then in half again widthwise. You will have a rectangle with a wedge marked at one corner four layers thick. (Think back to those paper snowflakes made in elementary school.) Cut along the traced line to make one circle that will fit into the bottom of your pan. Take the paper left from cutting the circle and cut all the way across a fold line to form two pieces. Use these pieces to shield a cake plate from frosting by lining the plate with the curved side next to the cake.

# macaroon drops

EVEN THOUGH I'VE USED IT THROUGHOUT THIS COOKBOOK, the time has come for me to admit that, as much as I love it and use it, coconut is a polarizing ingredient in America. In fact, it consistently ranks as one of the five most polarizing foods, and studies have actually revealed that out of a box of lovely assorted chocolate candy, the one with coconut is most likely to be eaten last. Of course, this horrifies me! Coconut is one of the most predominant crops produced in Kerala, and we use it in both sweet and savory dishes. Needless to say, I was glad to discover that when it comes to coconut, people in the Deep South are more forgiving and generally come down firmly on the love side rather than the hate side of the ingredient. I believe that residents of the Southeast, home to so many port cities, have always viewed coconut as a rather exotic, fancy ingredient because it arrived from such faraway places as the Philippines, India, and Brazil.

Coconut macaroons—not to be confused with the macaron, that dainty, brightly colored, and airy French cookie—that are commercially prepared often present as dense, moist, and overly sweet. But home cooks and skilled bakers tend to turn out more light and fluffy macaroons that showcase the macerated coconut, and this quick and deliciously chewy cookie does just that. Although coconut now abounds, the flavor remains exotic. Regardless of whether you love coconut or hate it, I think this recipe will bring you to my side. These macaroons pair well with Ginger Coffee (page 55).

**MAKES 24 MACAROONS**

2 cups sweetened, dried coconut flakes

2 cups sweetened condensed milk

1½ teaspoons freshly grated nutmeg

1 teaspoon pure vanilla extract

2 large eggs, whites only

¼ teaspoon kosher salt

Heat the oven to 325°F. Line a baking sheet pan with parchment paper.

Combine the coconut, condensed milk, nutmeg, and vanilla in a medium bowl.

In an electric mixer using the whisk attachment, whip the egg whites and salt on high speed just until stiff peaks are formed. Carefully fold the coconut mixture into the whipped egg white mixture.

Using a 1½-inch-diameter ice-cream scoop, form about 24 macaroon drops and bake until golden brown, about 25 to 30 minutes.

**NOTES:** *These delectable coconut drops freeze well for up to a month; thaw and enjoy.*

# peanut sesame blondies *with* chocolate chunks

I'M A FOOL FOR A ROAD TRIP. The little picnic area beneath the World's Largest Peanut Monument in Ashburn, Georgia, is a superb place to stop and stretch your legs while the kids take selfies. I thought I might as well do my part to help Georgia's reputation as the premier land of the peanut, so I set about developing a portable, packable version of the classic snack commonly known as blondies. Already chock-full of peanuts and peanut butter, I added chocolate chips for my son and toasted sesame seeds for me. The result is a protein-packed snack that will please peanut lovers everywhere.

MAKES 16 BARS

8 tablespoons (1 stick) unsalted butter, melted, plus more for greasing baking dish

1 cup packed light-brown sugar

2 large eggs

1 teaspoon pure vanilla extract

1/2 cup (4 ounces) creamy peanut butter

1/4 teaspoon kosher salt

1/2 teaspoon baking powder

1 cup unbleached all-purpose flour

1 tablespoon sesame seeds, toasted, divided

1/2 cup (4 ounces) roasted salted peanuts, roughly chopped and divided

1/2 cup (4 ounces) bittersweet chocolate chips, divided

Heat the oven to 350°F. Grease an 8 x 8-inch baking dish and set aside.

Using an electric mixer, combine the melted butter and light-brown sugar by beating at medium speed for 1 minute. Add in the eggs one at a time, beating well after each, then add the vanilla extract and beat on medium speed for another 30 seconds. Add in the peanut butter and beat for another 2 minutes; scrape the bottom and sides of the bowl to make sure all of the ingredients are thoroughly mixed. Add the salt, baking powder, and flour, and beat on low speed until the ingredients are well combined and the batter is thick and smooth, about 2 minutes. Let mixture sit and cool for a minute or two. Add 1 1/2 teaspoons of the sesame seeds, 1/4 cup of the peanuts, and 1/4 cup of the bittersweet chocolate chips; mix, on low, for another 30 seconds.

Evenly spread the batter into the baking dish using a plastic spatula. Sprinkle the remaining sesame seeds, peanuts, and chocolate chips on top and gently press them into the surface of the batter.

Bake until a toothpick inserted in the middle comes out with cakey crumbs attached, about 20 to 25 minutes.

**NOTES:** *These bars keep well in an airtight container for one week or well wrapped and frozen for three months.*

# apple pie *with* jaggery cumin drizzle

APPLE PIE IS NOT A FAMILIAR DESSERT IN INDIA. We use apples in other recipes but seldom in baked goods. Yet I grew up aware that apple pie was the quintessential American dessert. Needless to say, when we first arrived in America, one of the first desserts I tried was a slice of good ol' apple pie. When we lived in New York City, each fall we would travel with friends and family out into the country on apple-picking expeditions. Those drives were as memorable and colorful as my aunt's mango cellar back in Kerala: the leaves were awash in bright yellow, orange, rust, and various shades of red. The crisp air lent a sense of anticipation to the visits, and the most exciting part of it all was knowing that once back in the city, I got to bake apple pies. Before I became a southerner, I was an American, and nothing makes me feel it more than this most American of desserts. This recipe is the familiar fresh apples spiced with cinnamon and ginger but served with a drizzle of melted jaggery and piquant cumin.

**MAKES ONE 9-INCH PIE**

1 Cream Cheese Piecrust (page 39)

5 to 6 medium Granny Smith apples (about 2 pounds), peeled, cored, and sliced into thick wedges

1/2 cup (4 ounces) shaved jaggery

1 teaspoon cinnamon powder

1/2 teaspoon cumin seeds

2 tablespoons unbleached all-purpose flour

Heat the oven to 350°F. Dust a rolling pin and work surface lightly with flour. Divide the dough and roll each half into a circle, with a uniform thickness of 1/4 inch and a diameter of 10 inches. Line a 9-inch pie pan with one dough circle; set aside the other.

In a large bowl, combine apple slices with jaggery, cinnamon, cumin, and flour. Place apple mixture in pie shell.

Place second piecrust round on top. Fold the edges under and crimp to seal. Cut 4 small slits in the top crust to allow for steam to release as the pie bakes. Bake the pie until filling is bubbly and top crust is golden brown, approximately 40 minutes. Remove the pie from the oven and brush with the Jaggery Cumin Drizzle. Serve slices of pie with additional sauce, if desired.

## JAGGERY CUMIN DRIZZLE

4 tablespoons (1/2 stick) unsalted butter

1 teaspoon cumin seeds, coarsely ground

1/3 cup (2 ounces) jaggery

In a small pan over low heat, melt the butter; add the cumin and stir constantly until you smell the aroma of the cumin seeds, about 30 seconds. Add the jaggery and 2 tablespoons of water. Continue to cook the sauce over low heat until the jaggery melts, about 3 minutes.

# crumble-topped chili-flake peach pie

MANY YEARS AGO, much to the embarrassment of Georgia, South Carolina became the largest peach-producing state in the South. Although car tags across my state carry the image of a peach as a symbol of Georgia, the truth is more than one town in South Carolina can rightly claim the title of "Peach Capital of the World." That said, folks in Georgia and South Carolina enjoy a little heated competition, whether they are rooting for the University of Georgia Bulldogs or the University of South Carolina Gamecocks—or Georgia peaches or South Carolina peaches. But one thing is for sure: when it comes to pie, everyone agrees that peach is the best.

Once our regulars at Spice to Table became accustomed to the heated undercurrents in our desserts, they began to clamor for an additional bite of heat in the peach pie. I suppose like in SEC football or peach cultivation, everyone warms to the excitement of competition. My answer to their fervor is this brown-sugared sweet peach pie fired up with candied ginger and red pepper flakes and an almond gingersnap crust.

## GINGERSNAP CRUST

30 gingersnap cookies (2 cups), finely crushed

1 1/2 cups almond flour

8 tablespoons (1 stick) unsalted butter, melted

Heat the oven to 350°F.

Place the gingersnap crumbs and almond flour in a large bowl and drizzle in the melted butter. Using your hands, mix thoroughly until the crumbs retain their shape when squeezed together, taking care that the mixture is not too dry or too wet. It should have the consistency of good sandcastle sand. Add a bit of butter if too dry and a bit more almond flour if too wet.

Press the crumbs tightly into a 9-inch pie plate and bake the piecrust until deep brown, about 15 minutes. Remove from the oven and set aside to cool while preparing the pie filling.

## PEACH FILLING

1½ tablespoons unsalted butter

6 large firm ripe peaches, peeled and thinly sliced, or frozen peaches, thawed (about 2½ pounds or 5 cups)

¾ cup white granulated sugar

1 teaspoon crushed red pepper flakes

1 teaspoon freshly grated nutmeg

1 tablespoon finely chopped, candied ginger (see notes)

4 tablespoons unbleached all-purpose flour

In a large skillet over medium heat, melt the butter and add the peaches, sugar, red pepper flakes, nutmeg, candied ginger, and flour. Cook over medium-low heat, stirring from time to time, until the liquid is thick. Be sure to not stir too vigorously so that the sliced peaches stay intact. Set aside to cool while preparing the topping.

Pour the peaches into the baked gingersnap piecrust. Spread the crumble topping evenly over the top of the peaches. Bake at 350°F, or until the topping is golden brown, about 30 to 35 minutes. Cool on a cooling rack for at least 45 minutes before slicing.

**NOTES:** *I always thought I knew how to pit a peach, but a longtime Georgia cook showed me otherwise. It would seem logical to follow the natural groove in the fruit, but that's the wrong approach. To pit a peach, cut around the peach at 90 degrees to the crease line, then cut pole to pole. It pops right open to reveal the pit.*

*Candied ginger or crystallized ginger is fresh ginger root that has been boiled in a sugar syrup then coated with coarse sugar. It can be found in the spice aisle in little jars or in specialty markets and baking sections. Don't confuse it with preserved ginger, which has been cured with salt and sugar.*

## CRUMBLE TOPPING

1 cup unbleached all-purpose flour

½ cup packed dark-brown sugar

6 tablespoons (¾ stick) unsalted butter, cut into ¼-inch pieces, cold

Using a pastry blender or fingertips, combine the ingredients until crumbly and slightly moistened throughout.

# payasam *or* sweet coconut lentil soup *with* sultanas *and* cashews

THROUGHOUT THIS BOOK I HAVE SHARED THOUGHTS about classic southern, or American, recipes, so I have to add that if there is ever was a quintessential dessert in Kerala, it would be this yellow lentil *payasam*. Traditionally, this recipe entails an all-day process. My great-aunt Rita Netto would spend hours over this dish, making each component from scratch. She would constantly be stirring, even letting the telephone go unanswered if she was involved in its preparation. It seemed like tedious work, yet she was always smiling, happy to be making this dessert for one celebration or another—as the impending gathering meant the arrival of her twenty-five to thirty great-nieces and -nephews. This version is specific to Kerala and is another version of *kheer*. However, unlike the previous *kheer* dessert recipe that calls for vermicelli, this one uses golden lentils as the base. I have simplified this recipe for modern life, knowing that few of us have the sort of time, much less dedication, which my dear Valliammi dedicated to hers. I realize that it may seem strange to use lentils in a sweet dessert soup, but their mild taste and creamy consistency provide the perfect base for a stunningly delicious recipe. So, yet again, trust me on this; you are going to love it!

# PAYASAM *with* SULTANAS *and* CASHEWS

3 tablespoons ghee, divided

1/2 cup (4 ounces) dried yellow lentils, rinsed and picked over for debris

1 1/2 cups (12 ounces) cane syrup

2 cups coconut milk

1/4 cup (2 ounces) golden seedless raisins or sultanas

1/4 cup (2 ounces) raw cashews

Heat 2 tablespoons of the ghee in a medium saucepan over medium heat and add the yellow lentils, cooking until the lentils become a golden brown, about 2 minutes. Add 2 cups water and cook, partially covered, over moderate heat, lifting the lid and stirring occasionally, until the lentils are tender, about 20 minutes (add additional time if necessary to make sure the lentils are tender before proceeding). When the lentils have reached the desired consistency, add the cane syrup and cook over low heat, stirring constantly, for about 5 minutes. At this point, the mixture should be nice and thick. Add the coconut milk and stir well, and continue cooking, stirring constantly over low heat, for another 5 minutes or until the lentil mixture bubbles like molten lava and the lentils coat the spoon. Remove the pan from the heat.

In a small skillet over medium-high heat, add the remaining ghee, raisins, and cashews; then stir constantly until the cashews are slightly golden brown, about 2 minutes.

Spoon the raisins and cashews over the *payasam* and serve warm.

**NOTES**: *This lentil dessert is a wonderful conclusion to a vegetarian meal and a key part of Onam, a unique ancient festival celebrated in Kerala. Onam is held each fall to celebrate the rice harvest, which also coincides with several other significant cultural and religious traditions. During Onam, we eat a celebration harvest meal, the Onam sadya, which showcases twenty-one or more vegetarian dishes, served with great care on banana leaves. Payasam is the dish served to conclude this elaborate meal. Of course, the dishes could be served the modern way on plates, but Keralans strictly adhere to the time-consuming ritual and manner of presentation.*

*According to the story of Onam, a king called Mahabali once ruled Kerala. He was a wise, benevolent, and judicious ruler and beloved of his subjects. It is said that there was perfect equality, peace, and happiness in his kingdom, and Mahabali's fame as an able king began to spread far and wide. But the gods grew envious of his acts of benevolence and growing popularity. Presuming that he might become overpowerful, the gods decided to put Mahabali to a test. Lord Vishnu, one of the gods, transformed himself into a dwarf and approached Mahabali, asking for alms. Mahabali was pleased and impressed by the dwarf's wisdom and granted him a wish.*

*The dwarf asked for a simple gift—the amount of land he could measure in three paces—and the king agreed to it. The dwarf then increased his stature, and with the first step, he covered the sky, blotting out the stars, and with the second, he straddled the netherworld. Realizing that the third step would destroy the earth, Mahabali offered his head as the last step.*

*The lord Vishnu took the fatal third step and pushed Mahabali into the netherworld, but before he was banished forever, the gods, moved by his love for his people, granted him a boon. Mahabali asked that he be allowed to return once a year from exile to visit his people. Onam celebrates the homecoming of King Mahabali. Whether Hindu, Muslim, Christian, or Jew, grateful Keralans pay a glorious tribute to the memory of this benevolent king who gave his all for his subjects by celebrating Onam.*

*The sadya meal is served to everyone who enters your home that day, regardless of background, religion, or status in life. This meal is a perfect example of why I feel such kinship with the American South: the art of hospitality is ingrained in my cultural DNA and is in sync with the hospitality and warmth I have found all over the American South.*

*This payasam is the culinary equivalent of the sweet embrace of my two Souths.*

# acknowledgments

## FROM ASHA

My agent, Janis Donnaud, who found me and believed as I do that I had a story to tell and share with the world. My writer, Martha Foose, who walked me through this process with care and inspiration, pushing me out of my comfort zone and helping me reach deeply into my own memories to find stories that connected the dots. Jennifer Kasius, my editor at Running Press, who allowed me to stay true to my story and vision for this book. Susan Van Horn, the book designer, for her creative genius. Evan Sung for his uncanny ability to bring food to life through the magic of photography. Kate Mueller's editorial acumen is greatly appreciated. Thomas Diver, our stylist, who understood my southern sensibility. Chef Anne Quatrano whose culinary genius has been a source of inspiration and everything I continue to aspire to be as a chef. Chef Vishwesh Bhatt for paving the path and articulating the connections between India and the American South. My friends David Moody and Martin Mans for being my extended family and the family I had the pleasure of choosing to be in my circle. My deepest appreciation to Anne Vincent, for giving me the gift of my nephew, Marcus Gomez, who has enriched my life in infinite ways. I will be eternally grateful to Bobby Palayam for being my best friend and the most amazing father to our son, Ethan. I thank my son, Ethan, for allowing me to experience love, laughter, and purpose in its most pure form and for being my raison d'etre. And finally my mother, Hazel Gomez, I thank for the joys her kitchen brought to my life and for the unending memories that ignited my love affair for food, tradition, and innovation.

## FROM MARTHA

I thank our agent, Janis Donnaud, a whole heck of a lot for having faith in my work and coupling me up with Asha for this project. Ramone, thanks for doing your job. Jayne Kennedy and Minter Byrd—I would be lost without y'all as friends. Sister Yolande Van Heerden, thanks for all the distractions. My mother, Cindy Foose, is a model of grace, and I thank her every hour for all she has done for me. Donald and Joe Bender, you two fellows mean the world to me.

# metric conversions

The recipes in this book have not been tested with metric measurements, so some variations might occur. Remember that the weight of dry ingredients varies according to the volume or density factor: 1 cup of flour weighs far less than 1 cup of sugar, and 1 tablespoon doesn't necessarily hold 3 teaspoons.

## GENERAL FORMULA FOR METRIC CONVERSION

Ounces to grams ....................... multiply ounces by 28.35

Grams to ounces........................ multiply ounces by 0.035

Pounds to grams ....................... multiply pounds by 453.5

Pounds to kilograms.................... multiply pounds by 0.45

Cups to liters ........................... multiply cups by 0.24

Fahrenheit to Celsius .............. subtract 32 from Fahrenheit temperature, multiply by 5, divide by 9

Celsius to Fahrenheit .............multiply Celsius temperature by 9, divide by 5, add 32

## VOLUME (LIQUID) MEASUREMENTS

1 teaspoon = 1/6 fluid ounce = 5 milliliters

1 tablespoon = 1/2 fluid ounce = 15 milliliters

2 tablespoons = 1 fluid ounce = 30 milliliters

1/4 cup = 2 fluid ounces = 60 milliliters

1/3 cup = 2 2/3 fluid ounces = 79 milliliters

1/2 cup = 4 fluid ounces = 118 milliliters

1 cup or 1/2 pint = 8 fluid ounces = 250 milliliters

2 cups or 1 pint = 16 fluid ounces = 500 milliliters

4 cups or 1 quart = 32 fluid ounces = 1,000 milliliters

1 gallon = 4 liters

## VOLUME (DRY) MEASUREMENTS

1/4 teaspoon = 1 milliliter

1/2 teaspoon = 2 milliliters

3/4 teaspoon = 4 milliliters

1 teaspoon = 5 milliliters

1 tablespoon = 15 milliliters

1/4 cup = 59 milliliters

1/3 cup = 79 milliliters

1/2 cup = 118 milliliters

2/3 cup = 158 milliliters

3/4 cup = 177 milliliters

1 cup = 225 milliliters

4 cups or 1 quart = 1 liter

1/2 gallon = 2 liters

1 gallon = 4 liters

## WEIGHT (MASS) MEASUREMENTS

1 ounce = 30 grams

2 ounces = 55 grams

3 ounces = 85 grams

4 ounces = 1/4 pound = 125 grams

8 ounces = 1/2 pound = 240 grams

12 ounces = 3/4 pound = 375 grams

16 ounces = 1 pound = 454 grams

## LINEAR MEASUREMENTS

1/2 in = 1 1/2 cm

1 inch = 2 1/2 cm

6 inches = 15 cm

8 inches = 20 cm

10 inches = 25 cm

12 inches = 30 cm

20 inches = 50 cm

## OVEN TEMPERATURE EQUIVALENTS, FAHRENHEIT (F) AND CELSIUS (C)

100°F = 38°C

200°F = 95°C

250°F = 120°C

300°F = 150°C

350°F = 180°C

400°F = 205°C

450°F = 230°C

# recipes by category

## SOUPS AND STEWS

## BREADS

## SANDWICHES

## GRAINS AND RICE

## CONDIMENTS AND SAUCES

## SAVORY AND SWEET PIES, COBBLER, AND TART

## FISH AND SEAFOOD

## VEGETABLE DISHES: (v) = vegetarian

# index

Note: Page references in *italics* indicate photographs.